WESTMAR COLLEGE

W9-CBX-424

COMPUTERS
IN THE
CLASSROOM

The Advisory Panel

Roberta O. Anderson, Media Coordinator, Grandview Elementary School, Provo, Utah

John C. Arch, sixth grade teacher, Park Avenue School, Nashville, Tennessee

Rosetta Johnson-Taylor, sixth grade teacher and Intermediate Coordinator, Frank Zervas School, Newton, Massachusetts

Jean B. Rogers, Instructor, Department of Computer and Information Science, University of Oregon, Eugene

John J. Tzeng, Professor and Director of Media-TV Lab, University of the District of Columbia, Washington

Computers in the Classroom

Henry S. Kepner, Jr.
Editor

Foreword by
Bruce E. Brombacher
1982 National Teacher of the Year

National Education Association
Washington, D.C.

LB
1028.5
.C573
1982

Copyright © 1982
National Education Association of the United States

Stock No. 1825-7-00

Note

The opinions in this publication should not be construed as representing the policy or position of the National Education Association. Materials published as part of the Developments in Classroom Instruction series are intended to be discussion documents for teachers who are concerned with specialized interests of the profession.

Library of Congress Cataloging in Publication Data

Main entry under title:

Computers in the classroom

(Developments in classroom instruction)
   1. Computer-assisted instruction. I. Kepner,
Henry S. II. Series
LB1028.5.C573 1982   371.3'9445   82-8121
ISBN 0-8106-1825-7   AACR2

101690

CONTENTS

Foreword

The microcomputer revolution is upon us. Almost every facet of our lives is impacted by the power of computers. On a daily basis we interact with automatic banking machines, computerized cash register systems, computer-controlled telecommunications systems, computer games, and many more computer-related devices. The tremendous growth of the computer industry and the increased accessibility of computers have caused a furor in the public sector.

Parents are buying microcomputers for their preschoolers. Students are saving money to purchase their own computers. Parent groups and community service organizations are donating many computers to the schools. Whether a $10,000 microcomputer system or a classroom set of pocket-sized $100 microcomputers, this equipment is in the schools to stay. The public attitude is "Here they are, now do something with them." The public wants immediate results. There is pressure to offer classes for children at all grade levels both during the school day and after school hours. Adults also want schools to offer evening and weekend programs. Everyone is looking to the schools for assistance in determining the computer's role in society.

As educators what can we do? Our professional associations have made computers an integral part of their recommendations for education in the 1980's and 1990's. Workshops, in-service sessions, and entire conferences are dedicated to the new computer technology and the impact it will have on the schools. However, the constraints of time and limited funds make it difficult to assimilate all the information and devise a comprehensive plan to implement computers in the classroom.

Our real need is to gain an overview of what computers are, what they can and cannot do for us, and most importantly, how they can be used effectively as an instructional tool in the classroom. All of this must be accomplished quickly, because in many cases the computers are in place waiting to be used.

5

This book attempts to meet the needs of educators who are trying to integrate computers into the classroom. It is a unique collection of articles written by authors who are on the leading edge of the computer movement in education. The articles provide an overview of computer technology, a summary of educational uses of computers, and descriptions of practical programs that can be easily implemented in many curricular areas.

For the novice computer-using educator, this book is an excellent introductory handbook. It provides step-by-step procedures for selecting microcomputers and buying software to get started. It gives an overview of the many educational uses of computers to help focus on the wide range of possibilities for integrating computers into the classroom. Finally, the book provides practical examples of instructional programs that are in place and working effectively to bring computers into the classroom. Novice users can take these model activities as a starting point for devising their own computer-enhanced lessons.

For the more experienced computer user, the book serves as a reference guide and a resource publication. It provides educators with an opportunity to compare model programs to the projects they have already developed and implemented in their own classrooms. This in turn may stimulate an exchange of ideas and assist in initiating improvements in the current programs offered in the curriculum.

This book will be very helpful to pre-service teachers, classroom teachers, in-service planners, teacher educators, and administrators, as well as to parents and others who are dedicated to providing exciting and meaningful instruction using computers in the classroom.

Bruce E. Brombacher
Mathematics Teacher and Department Chairperson
Jones Junior High School, Upper Arlington, Ohio
1982 National Teacher of the Year

Introduction

Computers are here for the schools. Are teachers ready? Over the next decade the computer will become a valuable tool in the schools, just as it has already become in business, industry, and government. Why the sudden rush to put computers in the classroom? There are three major reasons: (1) the development of instructional uses for computers, (2) technological advances and financial accessibility through the microcomputer revolution, and (3) extreme student interest in and curiosity about interacting with computers.

This book provides an introduction to computer uses—current and planned—for classroom instruction. The articles are not uniform in length or computer development because the use of the computer for instruction has been explored unevenly in the various disciplines. And although the computer has many uses in the school, this book focuses on instructional uses rather than on recordkeeping, budget, and management. The book is divided into three parts: Educational Uses of Computers, The Computer in the Curriculum, and Computer Equipment and Materials.

In the first article, "Instructional Applications of Computers," Dennis delineates the range of instructional applications that computers can serve. A thorough study of these applications will help teachers use the computer as a classroom tool. Too many applications fail because they are used for tasks that the computer cannot be expected to perform effectively. Articles by Klassen and Rawitsch, Hynek and Schluter, Tenison, O'Connor, Kmoch, Hausmann, and the editor spell out examples of instructional applications in specific curriculum areas—language arts and reading, social studies, fine arts, business education and careers, science, middle school mathematics, senior high school mathematics—and also in the elementary school.

A major shortcoming of computers in the classroom today is the lack of well-developed instructional software (that is, computer programs written to direct students). In her article, "Computer Software in Education," Edwards addresses this deficiency and describes positive steps for writing and disseminating instructional programs.

In addition to using computers, students need to know about them as a tool in society. In the article "Computer Literacy," Klassen and Anderson identify the major student understandings as well as the computer uses. And in the article "Computer Science: A Secondary School Course," Kmoch and Kepner address the study of computer science as a discipline.

The second factor responsible for the rapid introduction of computers in the classroom is the technological advances in microcomputers and their financial accessibility. The history of computers is short and phenomenal. The first electronic computers, built in the 1940's, were accessible to only the world's top scientists. Then, about 1965, the first computer to sell for under $1 million was marketed. Today, an individual can purchase a small general-purpose computer for personal, business, or educational uses in the $1-thousand range.

As a consequence of technological development, access, and costs, some universities initiated instructional computing in the 1960's. Computing began to infiltrate secondary schools in the early 1970's in the form of terminals connected via telephone lines to a time-sharing computer at a remote site—a university, a local industry, or an administration building. Although the number of schools with computer access grew dramatically during the 1970's, the typical secondary school had only one terminal or a small number of terminals. Thus, computer access was usually available to only a few highly motivated students.

The introduction of hobbyist computers and subsequent home computers, such as the Commodore PET, the Tandy Radio Shack TRS-80, and the Apple II, made school use practical and affordable. Despite great potential, however, these computers do not have unlimited capabilities. McClain and Thomas in their article, "Selecting Microcomputers for the Classroom," present major questions for school personnel to consider when purchasing this equipment.

The third major reason for inclusion of computers in the classroom is student and parent awareness of computers as a part of the environment. Many students and parents are aware of, if not addicted to, the Atari television games and other computerized challenges. Although many of these popular games focus on psychomotor skills, most have educational value. It is important that teachers avoid rejecting computer games just because their learning outcomes are not those charged to the schools. Albrecht, Burton, and Zamora discuss the pervasiveness of computers in everyday experiences in

8

their article, "Computertown, U.S.A."

Today, business leaders, astronauts, sociologists, airline pilots, politicians, and others learn through simulation activities. The traditional classroom has seldom used simulation as an instructional strategy, however. In the article "Computer Games: An Educational Tool Beyond Compare," Ahl addresses the use of simulation activities as one of the most effective instructional techniques available. Since this technique is often best suited to individual or small group learning that requires immediate feedback, it is one that the computer can easily bring to the classroom, resource center, or laboratory. Klassen and Rawitsch, in "The Computer in the Social Studies," cite the value of simulations in that curriculum area.

Today, many students have the ability to learn more because of computer-related technology. In "The Computer and Exceptional Children," the editor cites some ways in which computers help handicapped as well as gifted individuals receive information, respond to their environment, and communicate with others more effectively.

The computer will have a profound impact on the schools but it will not replace the teacher. It will carry out some of the routine tasks with children, thus freeing the teacher for more meaningful student contact. It will provide more alternatives for instruction and more detailed records of student performance in skills and other tasks. In its best use, the computer will provide information to teacher, student, and parent for effective decisionmaking in the educational process.

Henry S. Kepner, Jr.

The Editor

Henry S. Kepner, Jr., is Professor of Curriculum and Instruction at the University of Wisconsin–Milwaukee, where he is responsible for computer and mathematics education. A former mathematics teacher in grades 7–12, his experience also includes teaching computer science to elementary, junior high, and high school students, and conducting in-service computer education courses for teachers. He is a co-author of *Reading in the Mathematics Classroom*, published by NEA.

1.   Instructional Applications of Computers

J. Richard Dennis

One of the major activities of a school is instruction. For computers to be of benefit to classrooms, their value as an aid to instruction must be apparent. There are several ways to derive such benefits. One way is to use the computer to provide a type of instruction (or potential learning) otherwise impossible or practical to provide. Another way is to have the computer assume roles or responsibilities of a very routine but necessary nature, thus freeing the trained human to engage more fully in more complex, less regular, but equally necessary, parts of the activity.

This article describes a variety of ways in which computers have been successfully applied to instruction. Some provide routine services; some are designed to release teachers to engage more intensively in distinctively human aspects of instruction.

A computer can be used for instruction either as a medium of delivery, or as the topic itself. In the former case, computer teachers are teaching *with* a computer. In the latter case, they are teaching *about* computers.

TEACHING WITH A COMPUTER

A computer can become a medium of instruction or instructional support in a variety of ways. Descriptions of these ways follow, together with some of the influences of each style on the teacher's role and behavior. A full understanding of each use and the benefit to teacher or instruction greatly depends upon firsthand experiences with a well-designed computer system operating in a particular style.

Drill and Practice

One of the first instructional activities to be computerized was repeated student exercises to assist learning, an activity similar to the homework assignments of many teachers and to the exercise sets of many textbooks. The computer can be programmed not only to present exercises, but also to check the student's answer immediately

11

and to give a response based upon specifics of the answer. Textbooks cannot provide such services to students. Although correct answers can be printed in the back of a book, in text form it is difficult to give corrective messages to a wide variety of likely incorrect answers. In theory at least, the computer can do this. It can provide as many corrective messages to as many incorrect responses to a question as the creator of the lesson can invent or as teaching experience can provide.

This dependence upon the creativity of computer lesson writers was a problem in early drill-and-practice efforts. In fact, some may argue that the inadequacy of these early efforts seriously delayed the development of instructional computing. This is a matter for historians to decide. What is important now is to know that through experience, and by following a few basic principles of practice design, one can create computerized practice materials that greatly optimize the student's practice efforts. Primitively designed computer drills are not very attractive to good teachers nor, for regular use, to students.

Some of the principles of effective drill-and-practice design are as follows:

1. A correct answer to an exercise has only a small probability of indicating learning.
2. Several correct responses to an exercise, spread over time, increase the probability that learning has occurred. However, if the exercise recurs identically, there is an increasing danger that the learning is rote memorization.
3. Correct responses over time to a set of related but different exercises on a topic increase still more the probability that learning has taken place, rather than that a correct response has been memorized.
4. When the student makes incorrect responses, the student requires some form of corrective intervention. The more specific the intervention to the misconception causing the incorrect response, the more helpful it is to the student.
5. Variations of exercises on which errors occur need to be presented more often thereafter than those on which success regularly occurs.

The basic element of effective practice (the exercise) is usually in the form of a question or a directive requiring a student response. To successfully computerize the activity, one must pay careful attention to many more facets of an exercise. What is needed is the concept called "the questioning episode" (1). A well-designed, computerized questioning episode should include the following ingredients:

1. An interrogative or directive expression, perhaps accompanied by other statements
2. An opportunity and a requirement for student response (input)
3. A means of computer interpretation of the student's input that accurately distinguishes among
   a. All conceivable correct replies
   b. All conceptually correct but literally incorrect replies
   c. All likely-to-occur incorrect replies
   d. Unidentifiable replies
4. A set of computer-offered consequences or remarks specific to each of the student's inputs
5. A decision algorithm to establish a duration to the practice event.

The ability of a question episode to interpret and classify student answers provides one of the important measures of individualization. Particularly on constructed answer exercises, there are usually many ways to respond correctly. And there are several more ways to be "thinking correctly, but saying it wrong." Misspellings fall into this category. Then there is the distinction between an incorrect answer for which "I think I know why you answered that way" and one for which "I haven't the faintest notion what you are thinking." The completeness and accuracy with which a question episode makes these distinctions greatly influence the quality of the episode. In fact, it is very possible that deficiencies of this type in the early attempts at drill and practice disenchanted many potential advocates of the medium.

In a truly interactive instructional environment, more than mere knowledge of correctness or incorrectness is appropriate. The replies that are given to confirm or reject an answer can include much teaching. For computerized exercises replies should contain at least the following:

1. Messages that confirm correct answers and reinforce reasons for the correctness
2. Messages that confirm correct thinking when detected and facilitate construction of a literally correct answer

3. Messages that inform of predictable incorrect answers and give reasons for the incorrectness that will facilitate a remedy
4. Messages that inform of unidentifiable incorrect answers and suggest appropriate means of seeking help in remedying the situation

Clearly this part of a question episode is intimately tied to the input interpretation provision of the episode. Good computerized instruction should go to great lengths to avoid: (1) a no to an alternate form of the correct answer, (2) a no to an incorrect answer with no hint of why it is incorrect, (3) an OK to answers that appear correct but may have been derived accidentally because of a misconception.

Despite Herculean efforts to carefully design corrective measures and individual responses, there will be occasional students who, for some exercises, answer incorrectly time after time, and for whom the corrective measures do not alter the situation. In such cases the computer must decide how long to permit the situation to continue and how to end it. Students who, for whatever unknown reason, believe their answer to be correct and continue giving it, while the computer continues to reject it, can become very frustrated and their motivation and interest can be destroyed very quickly. All question episodes require a means of limiting these "endless loops" when they occur—such as a limit on the number of responses that are permitted. Beyond this, there should be careful attention to what the computer does when these situations occur. The inability to answer correctly may prevent students from successfully continuing to the next exercise. Perhaps they should go back through specific episodes to attempt to construct knowledge that is either missing or incorrectly constructed, or perhaps the appropriate decision is to terminate the session. The important point is that whenever such a discontinuity occurs, the teacher must somehow be informed of the details. This can be achieved by instructing students to consult the teacher with some form of record (such as a paper copy) of their experiences, or by putting a data profile of the experiences into a computer file which the teacher can consult at a later time.

At present, it is rare to find computer materials in which questioning occurs with so much detail. This is not because computers are incapable of doing such questioning; rather it is because so much human attention to material design is difficult and expensive. For future implementation of many materials in many subjects for many students, however, attention to such details will be necessary.

When sound design principles for computerized practice are followed, many annoying features found in early practice attempts will disappear and students will be provided helpful, motivating experiences. It is therefore important for teachers to know what constitutes well-designed practice materials and to accept nothing less.

The need for practice of such intensity varies from subject to subject. For example, mathematics, which requires mastery of a large number of computing facts and processes, requires frequent practice. One might predict that a school could never have the amount of computing equipment necessary to provide adequate practice to more than a few students. This has been the case, but it is rapidly changing as lower-cost computers continue to proliferate, and as teachers experiment and gain experience with this style of computer teaching. Some teachers use computerized drills as a means of aiding recovery of dulled prerequisites. Students needing such review use a computer communication device (or terminal) for a brief but intensive practice session. Alternatively, computer-using teachers opt to have computerized practice as a part of initial instruction and mastery achievement. To the extent permitted by available equipment, students engage in responsive computerized practice interspersed with the usual exercise activity.

Both styles of automated practice use in the the classroom benefit from well-designed practice facilities. Generally, students engaged in computerized practice are able to complete in a time period two to three times as many exercises as they complete in other practice modes. The computer has the effect of expediting their work.

Tutorials

Instructional computing in the tutorial style is an attempt to give the computer ability to stand alone in teaching situations. As every teacher knows, this is a very difficult task. Tutorial computer lessons, in a sense, are simulations of the best teaching behavior. Usually it is possible to recognize very good teaching in contrast to very bad. To identify all the ingredients and particularly the decisions of the acts for computer replication, however, is a monumental task. To do so, one must become acutely aware in an instructional episode of what is done, when, why, and for whom. Usually, not all of these variables are clearly or uniquely defined. Successful attempts at tutorial style computer instruction to date have been very few in number and very narrow in topic context.

Future successes in this style of instructional computing will require significant new developments in the design of computerized lessons, including techniques through which a computerized tutorial can "learn from its own teaching experience." Computer scientists have built computerized game-playing programs that learn from their play and, hence, improve with experience. Teaching programs will need similar talents.

Simulation

In many situations there is a phenomenon which is characterized by a task to be completed, a goal to be reached, or an environment to be understood. Frequently, completing the task, reaching the goal, or achieving the understanding requires correct execution of a variety of decisions, or correct interpretation of a variety of data. Many such phenomena involve a degree of risk or jeopardy of some form— for example, learning to fly an airplane, learning to perform particular (perhaps dangerous) laboratory procedures, learning to understand and control various social or physical phenomena such as environmental pollution or population growth, learning to diagnose diseases, and learning to manage a business.

Of course, there are textbooks for all these subjects which describe the principles of each phenomenon. When, in addition to acquired text knowledge, however, the desired learning includes a demonstration of performance, some means is needed to help the learner from the text knowledge to effective performance. Apprenticeships, carefully supervised by professionals, are one such means, but they greatly increase the costs of education and limit the audience to which such learning can be made available.

What is needed is a recreation of key parts of the actual environment to permit students to have surrogate experiences without the necessity of the real consequences of misjudgments. Such a recreation is a *simulation*. The extent to which a simulation causes the learner to identify with the situation, or to view his or her actions as real, is called the *fidelity* of the simulation. Not all simulations require a computer. Many are in paper-and-pencil form and many are in the form of board games. Role playing is another form of simulation.

In schools, simulations can make available to students environments that might not otherwise be accessible due to great expense, safety factors, or time requirements to experience important consequences. Types of simulation particularly popular in schools are those which replicate various laboratory procedures or experiments (acid/base titrations, identification of unknowns, breeding of organisms) or which permit experimentation with physical phenomena not easily available in the real world environment (execution of lunar landings, control of water pollution).

Simulations are expensive and difficult to build. In use, they tend to encourage multiple experiences by students, an aspect which can greatly increase classroom management problems. Educators are just beginning to understand what simulations do and how they do it in learning situations. Several have suggested that learning derived from simulation is different from that derived from other means. To date, studies of simulation have consistently demonstrated good learner attitudes about the experiences. Much more research is needed, however, to understand how simulation learning differs from other types of learning.

Instructional Games

Play has long been an important mode of learning. In play, a person is motivated and kept active on a task, and the task changes as a result of the person's activity. These are attributes of learning settings long favored by educators. As students grow older, however, play as a mode of intellectual learning becomes less noticeable in schools. This may be due in part to adult feelings that as one grows older, learning should become more like work, with fun replaced by, at best, "serious enjoyment" or detached satisfaction.

One of the challenging uses of computers has been attempts to enable individuals to participate in a variety of games. These games frequently find disfavor in schools because their specific learning is difficult to identify (and relate to the school curriculum). Certainly, as a result of many experiences with, say, a Star Wars game, students' behaviors do change. But it is difficult to say how those changes are related to school objectives.

A game is an activity involving individual decision and a competition over some limited commodity. When the performances of play involve acquisition of behaviors related to school objectives they are called "instructional games." Many such games have been computerized. Some have included the creation of a process permitting the computer to adjust its play ability to that of the student. Computerized simulations have been turned into games (simulation games) by adding competition to the decision activities of the user.

Almost every subject has instructional games available. In mathematics, one of the best known is Battleship, a game in which students practice the use of coordinates on a two-dimensional surface. Teachers of business courses frequently use the Executive Game to introduce students to decisions on production, marketing, finance, and competition. Teams of four students each organize as hypothetical companies which make a variety of business decisions as they compete with each other.

Problem Solving

Computers are used in problem solving activities in at least two ways: (1) with programs prepared by other sources and (2) with programs prepared by the user. When the problem solving algorithms are available from some other source, the student merely provides the computer with appropriate data to generate a solution. A common example is the frequent use of statistical programs to generate results for a research study. This kind of computer problem solving requires the least amount of user training. In many areas of the school curriculum the availability of such resources would permit students to pursue activities otherwise too inefficient or too difficult. Mathematics, for example, is full of situations requiring repeated evaluation of a particular function or formula for carefully selected values. When done by hand, such activities usually require large amounts of calculation. A computer program greatly expedites this kind of study.

The teacher wishing to conduct problem-solving exercises with preexisting programs must have good sources of such programs or must be able to create them. Often an advanced student can assist with this task. The teacher must also be able to integrate instruction on the use of such programs with lessons on the subject of the problem.

In the second method of using computers in problems solving, the student prepares the program that will do the work. This requires a great deal more knowledge on the part of the student—for example, the ability to create an algorithm for solving the problem and, it is hoped, some method of demonstrating that the algorithm gives reasonable results. Students who successfully solve a problem in this way will have significantly more knowledge of the problem and its controlling variables than they would have by other means.

The teacher who wishes students to write their own computer programs must ensure that the students know how to do so. Perhaps they learned the skill in a previous course taught by another teacher. If not, the teacher needs not only personal programming skill, but also an extensive background in teaching such skill to others efficiently. Despite these seemingly large demands on the teacher, problem solving is among the most frequent applications of computers in schools today.

Computer-Assisted Testing

Testing is one of the teacher's major activities. Although not one of the early activities to be attempted by computers, in recent years testing and evaluation have become one of the rapidly growing styles of computer activity in education. Several schemes for this type of computer use prevail, including computerized test grading, computer test item banking, computer test attribute banking, and test item generation.

Computerized test grading usually involves multiple choice or simple constructed response test items. The grading of sentence and essay-type responses is only partially within the means of instructional computer technology. In its simplest form, computerized grading provides checking of correct and incorrect answers, and tallying of student and class scores. More sophisticated systems include an array of statistical analyses of the student, the test, and the individual items. For the student, these may include a listing of incorrect responses together with correct answers, a raw score, a percentage score, a class rank, and so on. For the test, there may be a frequency distribution of student scores, an estimate of the test reliability, and also the more common mean, median, and standard deviation scores. For individual test items, there may be estimates of the item difficulty, the relative performance of the alternative choices (the distractors), and an estimate of the item's discrimination ability.

Providing lists of test or item statistics is of slight value if the teacher has little time for or experience in interpreting the results and acting on the interpretation. Sophisticated test grading systems will provide these interpretations wherever they are predictable. Informing the teacher that an item or alternative may be ambiguous, has an unexpected difficulty, or for some other reason needs rewriting is a service that saves time and encourages the teacher to systematically improve test efforts.

Computer *test item banking* is a scheme in which the computer stores, categorizes, and assists in the retrieval of test items. Such services have been pioneered by commercial testing services for standardized testing, and are finding increasing application in the more concentrated instructional settings such as universities, large schools, or large departments. Briefly, the computer stores each question and a variety of information concerning it (the objective it tests, its difficulty, the correct answers). In some systems, several items will be stored for each objective, giving a range or variety over

19

the other attributes. The computer then has a process that permits the teacher to specify the objectives a test is to measure, the number of items to include for each, the item difficulties, and so on. Some systems give the teacher an opportunity to accept or reject the items selected by the computer. Once approved, the test is produced by the computer, perhaps on a reproducible form. More sophisticated systems permit the teacher a variety of options for formatting the test or equivalent forms.

A computerized *item attribute banking system* is merely a subset of an item banking system. In this case only the attributes are in the computer. On request, identifying codes for appropriate items are listed. The teacher goes to a card file, a catalog, or other external medium to retrieve the actual items. This kind of system does not usually have test printing capabilities.

Sometimes a test grading system is coupled with an item or attribute banking system. In the better instances of such marriages, not only does the computer provide an array of grading services, but the item attributes are revised and updated each time the item is used on a test.

A *test item generating system* may also be coupled with the other computerized testing features to provide much richer varieties of test items. In this mode, the computer houses item forms (or templates). Each template is usually associated with a single objective and is used to generate as many items with as many variations as are built into the item pattern.

For use in schools, computer test grading and test analysis systems are the most readily implemented. For item banking systems, the teacher must either buy the items in the bank or write them. If several teachers of a course pool their test items, this can be efficient. Optimal use of computerized testing systems requires the teacher to have considerable knowledge—about computers (such as selecting storage devices large enough to do the job), and about testing and item construction, and some knowledge about computer software (such as the options and attributes of good computer testing programs).

Classroom Support

Every teacher has a myriad of routine activities to carry out that may relate to teaching only indirectly. Some may be greatly simplified with the aid of well-designed computer systems. In most cases, "well-designed" does not mean "large" or "expensive."

For example, one of the activities to which certain teachers must pay particular attention is the keeping of inventories. Science teachers, vocational teachers, home economics teachers, and business education teachers all keep up-to-date records of equipment and supplies. Coaches keep careful inventories of playing equipment and of individual players' performance statistics.

Each inventory requires essentially the same computer program to automate. With a little planning, a science teacher, say, can make an inventory that will not only keep track of how long each consumable should last, but upon request will give out a list of any items in low supply, together with the address of the supplier if ordering is necessary.

Another potentially powerful application of computers to schools is in the rapidly emerging field of word processing. This style of computer use can be implemented in any class that teaches composition or requires written course papers. A word processing facility automates the process of preparing and "massaging" a manuscript and permits students to act efficiently upon teacher critiques without having to laboriously recopy the entire paper.

The same facility is efficient for teachers to make fresh, legible copies of handouts used year after year. The text of a handout can be kept in a computer file. The incidental changes required to make it current (such as date changes) can be made quickly through the automated editing features of a computer. Even the smallest microcomputers have word processing programs (sometimes called text editors) that provide these services.

Computer-Managed Instruction (CMI)

In this style of instructional computing, the role of the computer is to control and expedite the "traffic" during instruction. In doing this, the computer assumes responsibility for tasks such as diagnosing, assigning, routing through the curriculum, communicating with members of the instructional setting, controlling and maximizing utilization of resources (such as time, equipment, instructional personnel), progress evaluation, and related recordkeeping.

Initial instruction may not be the responsiblity of the computer. The teacher may still conduct group lessons and discussions, and individual tutoring; but the computer may determine the need for such events, schedule them, and transmit information to the persons involved. The computer's objective is to keep each person in the instructional setting as productive as possible during a maximum portion of the time that the person chooses to devote to instructional tasks.

21

The tasks performed by a CMI system are essentially those needed to individualize instruction. This should not be construed, however, to mean that the teacher never works with groups nor gives instructional lectures. The difference is that with a good CMI system, group events occur on the basis of some identified need rather than on a regular schedule as in other settings. A group of students is determined to be ready for an introduction to or discussion of topic X, so the computer schedules it and announces it to the students involved.

In order to implement CMI in a course, the teacher's greatest needs are as follows:

1. A clearly defined curricular progression, including specification of points at which individual decisions must be made and the conditions for making each of them
2. A well-developed CMI control program, in which to embed the details of the curricular progression and all related decisions.

Several CMI systems have been developed and refined in recent years. The PLAN individualizing system developed by Westinghouse Learning Corporation and based in Iowa City, Iowa, provided no study management of an immediate variety. Rather, it administered study testing activities in a machine-readable form and transmitted student work to a central computer for evaluation. The system kept a record of student progress and, for each activity processed, issued an individual program of study which was reported to the participating school the next day.

The Advanced Instructional System (AIS) is one of several instructional management systems growing out of military training. Originated by McDonald-Douglas Corporation under a contract with the U.S. Air Force, the system was designed for large-scale instructional settings. It incorporates both interactive instruction and indirect managing techniques. The interactive terminals feature extensive graphics capabilities used by students in simulation activities and in adaptive testing. Under an adaptive testing model, the computer attempts to match question difficulty to the achievement level of the student. This system also includes management stations composed of an optical page reader and a printing device. This is the major control center for instruction, providing the student with answer grading services and with prescriptions for further study. Also, the system profiles student production of study to determine variation from a calculated "normal rate" of study.

The TICCIT system originally was developed by a team of researchers from the MITRE Corporation, a nonprofit research company, and from Brigham Young University. This system provides the user with a course authoring, delivery, and evaluation system for individualized instruction. An authoring language (called TAL) is used to prepare a wide variety of instructional styles, including questioning and simulation. Materials authoring has been structured to minimize the background required of the teacher. Other advanced CMI features of the TICCIT system include communication interactively or by computer mailbox, multimedia instructional control, extensive data gathering, and individual adaptation of instructional flow.

More recently, materials for microcomputers developed by many of the major materials publishers have included associated CMI systems for controlling and accounting for the interactions of students, computer, and the curriculum. Early efforts of this type have concentrated on elementary school mathematics and language arts skill objectives. Although some have reviewed the content of these efforts as simplistic, from an instructional management point of view the efforts clearly demonstrate that personal computers are more than capable of contributing to such schooling tasks. Again, the limitations perceived are the result of poor curriculum design, poor choice of instructional strategies, or unclear definition of objectives.

TEACHING ABOUT COMPUTERS

At precollege levels, the overwhelming majority of the activity has been to teach about the computer. Most of this effort has gone into teaching students to make a computer do what it will do, that is, *computer programming.* Sometimes teachers instruct students in detail on computer design and functions. Usually, however, this is a small portion of their effort.

An activity of growing importance in teaching about computers has come to be referred to as *computer literacy.* Essentially, this term refers to content under the heading of "what every person should know about computers." There are several views of what constitutes a computer literacy program, but usually the following topics are included:

1. Computer design and functioning survey
2. Uses of computers
3. The citizen and computers—personal rights, laws, and privacy issues involving computers

4. How humans control computers—an introductory programming experience.

There are three other common goals of teaching about computers. The first goal is the "preparation-for-college" objective prevalent in many other schooling activities. More and more undergraduate programs are including a basic understanding of computers and their uses in a particular field as a requirement for a degree. Precollege personnel argue for teaching about computers as a means of accelerating students when they reach college. The second goal, and one much less frequently articulated, is that of career education. Specifically, this refers to the goal of teaching entry-level job skills in some aspect of computing. This goal is clearly within the means of precollege programs. It is not uncommon among high schools with multiple course experiences in computing to have students take summer jobs or postgraduation positions as computer programmers. The third goal of teaching about computers is to provide important new learning skills to gain access to knowledge in a variety of other fields. The computer can be used to assist in gathering, organizing, and analyzing data in the solution of new problems.

Two common methods of computer use in teaching are *batch* style and *interactive* style computing. Batch style is usually done with computer-readable cards (the famous IBM cards). Programs are written on such cards either by using a keypunch machine to punch holes in the card to represent each letter or number, or by marking boxes on the card with a pencil. In many schools, the pencil marking of cards is preferred for batch style programming since it does not require additional expense for card punching equipment. Once a student program is recorded on the cards, it is presented to the computer through a reading device and the various results of the execution are reported through some kind of printing device.

For interactive style programming, a student creates a program by typing it on a keyboard of some form. Usually, the keyboard resembles a typewriter keyboard with added special-purpose keys. The student sees the results of the typing either on a piece of paper or on a display resembling a television screen. After constructing the program, the student uses the keyboard to instruct the computer to execute it. When it does so, the result appears on the paper or screen.

Interactive style programming gives the student more immediate results and usually makes for more efficient correction of errors in programming. It requires must greater investment in equipment to permit such activity by large numbers of students, however, since each student involved in a programming exercise ties up one keyboard-screen facility (or terminal) for her or his work. This tends to force compromise either in terms of the number of students who can enroll in such courses at a given time or in terms of the number of such activities each student can attempt. The batch style programming method, although less immediate, can handle much larger student loads with much less equipment since it usually requires the computer for only one or two minutes of the average 30-minute exercise.

Some computer "experts" may argue that batch style programming is an inferior experience for students. These arguments are matters of style and taste. The immediacy and efficiency of interactive computing is attractive. Schools that are trying to make such knowledge available to as many students as wish it, however, must frequently consider compromises on style or taste.

CONCLUSION

The main purpose of this article has been to assist the educator in obtaining an overview of instructional applications of computers. Although a large literature of techniques and research is associated with the field of educational computing, knowledge of this literature alone is not, in this author's opinion, an adequate background for an understanding of educational computing. The teacher also needs experience and experimentation with a variety of computer uses, from the viewpoint of both the student and the instructor.

Reference

1. Dennis, J. Richard. "The Question Episode—Building Block of Teaching with a Computer." Illinois Series on Educational Application of Computers, No. 4e. Champaign: Department of Secondary Education, University of Illinois, 1979.

2. Computer Literacy*

Daniel L. Klassen and Ronald E. Anderson

INTRODUCTION

During the past decade, computer technology has come to play a very important, often pivotal, role in American scientific, business, industrial, and governmental institutions. Efforts to improve productivity, increase efficiency and service, and to cope with the "information explosion" have spawned thousands of uses for computers. Our nation, it has been observed, has been transformed from an industrial society into an information society that relies heavily on computers and related information systems (11). According to a recent government report, the largest single class of employees in the United States today have jobs dealing, in the broadest sense, with information processing and communications, and it is well known that computer technology has influenced these areas extensively (45). In addition to the many known uses of computers, it is estimated that there are thousands of applications of the computer still awaiting discovery. As a recent *TIME* article put it, "Amazing feats of memory and execution become possible in everything from automobile engines to universities and hospitals, from farms to banks and corporate offices, from outer space to a baby's nursery" (15). To ask what these applications are is like asking what are the applications of electricity. There is little doubt, it seems, that life in the United States and in the rest of the industrial world, and eventually all over the planet, will be incalculably changed by computer technology.

NEED FOR COMPUTER LITERACY

In an information society such as ours, widespread understanding of computer technology and the consequences of computer use and

*This article was prepared with the support of National Science Foundation Grant No. SED 77–18658. Any opinions, findings, conclusions or recommendations expressed are those of the authors and do not necessarily reflect the views of the National Science Foundation.

misuse is necessary, even required, for public policymaking. A lack of understanding and acceptance of computers could seriously impede the use of computer technology in solving important problems. Many observers of the role of computer technology in society believe that if the gap between current technological capacity and the ordinary person's understanding of the technology is allowed to grow too wide, the social and political, as well as scientific, ramifications are likely to be very serious (36). Special concern about computers and information systems is justified because of their unique features and their close association with large bureaucratic institutions and the enterprise of science.

For the individual, an understanding of computer technology and uses is important because it reduces bewilderment about computers and promotes a balanced view of the computer's role in society. Such understanding also enables people to use and influence the design of computer-based social services and to develop informed opinions regarding particular computer applications having political, economic, and social implications.

Public understanding of computers and their applications has not kept pace with their availability and use. The AFIPS/TIME survey in 1971 showed that public attitudes are often unrealistic and negative, and understanding of computers is sometimes incorrect. The young, who have grown up in the "computer age" are not much better informed. The recently conducted Minnesota computer literacy study found that most junior and senior high students know very little about computers and their implications for society (27). Furthermore, most students do not understand the general limitations of computers. For instance, over half of the 1,500 students tested believe that "computers help people make decisions by providing correct answers to any question." Whereas those with no prior exposure to computers were more likely to give the incorrect response to this item, 43 percent of the students with computer programming experience also answered incorrectly. Answers to many other questions showed a similar lack of understanding and awareness. It is clear from this and other research (7) that students lack realistic views and basic knowledge of computers and that mere exposure to computers does not automatically eradicate misconceptions.

The growing recognition of the importance of widespread public understanding of computers in an information/computer society has prompted concerned educators to urge the launching of educational efforts to eliminate, or at least reduce, computer illiteracy. The President's Science Advisory Committee and the Organization for

Economic Cooperation and Development, in the late 1960's, were among the first groups to recognize the need to educate citizens. At about the same time, many educational and scientific societies also recognized this need. The International Federation of Information Processing Societies' Working Group in Secondary School Education, for instance, suggested that since it is important for all students to understand the nature and use of computers in modern society, teachers of all subjects should have a knowledge of computing. The Association of Computing Machinery's Elementary and Secondary Schools Subcommittee's Working Group on Computing Competencies for Teachers recently issued a similar plea (50). On several occasions, the Conference Board of Mathematical Sciences has also recommended the development of a computer literacy curriculum for precollege students (17); and in 1978, the National Council of Supervisors of Mathematics issued a position paper which included computer literacy for all citizens in a list of 10 basic skills. Most recently, the National Council for the Social Studies, in its position statement on curriculum, suggests that students be taught data processing skills.

In what is perhaps the most complete analysis of the importance of computer literacy, Andrew Molnar concludes that there is

> . . . a national need to foster computer literacy. Further, if we are to meet this need, we must ensure that high school graduates have an understanding of the uses and applications of the computer in society and its effect upon their everyday lives. . . . A nation concerned with its social needs and economic growth cannot be indifferent to the problems of literacy. If we are to reap the benefits of science-driven industries, we must develop a computer-literate society. (37)

DEFINITIONS OF COMPUTER LITERACY

Ten years ago "computer literacy" was a novel phrase, but now it is commonly used by educators, computer scientists, and journalists. Computer literacy has two major definitional roots: (1) the variety of specialized literacies, such as scientific literacy; and (2) general language literacy which encompasses reading, writing, and understanding. The conjunction of "computer" and "literacy" has had an intuitive appeal since communication with computers via computer language is analogous to interpersonal communication via ordinary language.

There are two generally accepted dictionary definitions of language literacy. One is the ability to communicate (for example, reading and writing); the other is the state of being informed, "cultured," and well versed. Although these definitions may be partially contradictory, the public continues to use the word literacy in these two ways. The descriptor "literate" is generally used to suggest a threshold on the literacy continuum. For instance, we might speak of a literate society as one where almost everyone can read and write. Or we might refer to a learned, knowledgeable, well-read person as literate. This discrepancy arises from "literate" meaning at times a "minimal" literacy level and at others meaning a very high literacy level.

The tradition of scientific literacy, and related forms such as technological literacy, economic literacy, and geographic literacy, to name only a few, suggests that the term literacy is mostly a matter of being informed rather than a communication skill. Both scientific literacy (44) and technological literacy have generally been defined as scientific and technical knowledge pertaining to social implications. Thus, for example, scientific literacy does not refer just to one's knowledge of biology but to one's understanding of the implications of biology, or more generally, the science-society interface. It is no wonder that in the computer literature the term computer literacy is equated with "computers and society."

We have proposed a definition of computer literacy which incorporates knowledge of computers, social implications of that knowledge, and also recognizes the need for skills in communicating with computers (3). Computer literacy, in our definition, is "whatever understanding, skills, and attitudes one needs to function effectively within a given social role that directly or indirectly involves computers." It should be clarified that we interpret "function effectively" within roles to be a matter of well-being and personal comfort, not just rational goal attainment. For the purpose of this article we apply the term "computer literacy" to the two most general roles—citizen and, by implication, student.

The school is the main institution for socialization in citizenship; thus, it is appropriate that computer literacy education be provided to future citizens as early as junior high school. It is imperative that students learn not only what every citizen needs to know about computers but what every student needs to know for doing effective schoolwork. The need to combine the computer education requirements of citizens and students implies that a broad spectrum of computer literacy is necessary. Students need to know how to use the computer as a tool in their schoolwork, and they need to know about the limitations, general capabilities, and social implications of computers for coping with computerization in their everyday lives.

This definition of computer literacy is quite compatible with most of the literature on the computer literacy concept. For instance, Moursund defined literacy as the "non-technical and low-technical aspects of the capabilities and limitations of computers, and of the social, vocational, and educational implications of computers" (41). This philosophy is effectively embodied in computer literacy texts for elementary students by Ball and Charp (10); and for secondary students by Billings and Moursund (13), and others. Those writing on the definition of computer literacy—for example, Rawitsch (47) and Thomas (51)—have expanded upon this approach to elaborate specific requirements in various arenas.

Our approach to computer literacy is broader than most. Some writers argue in favor of equating computer programming instruction with computer literacy (30). Others view computer literacy as just general knowledge about the role of computers in society. We believe that to function effectively as a citizen in the 1980's and beyond, one needs to know about the role of computers in society; and to function effectively as a student (in high school and above), one needs to know the elementary concepts and techniques of computer programming. Thus, a true computer literacy program should include these social elements as well as whatever else is needed to understand and be able to use computers in some minimal and meaningful way.

COMPUTER LITERACY OBJECTIVES

Our objectives for computer literacy are listed as an appendix to this article. The list of objectives is categorized into eight areas or domains and these are summarized as follows:

1. APPLICATIONS. This area covers the multitude of social and organizational areas into which computers have been integrated. It also covers the general considerations for applying computers to new situations.
2. HARDWARE. This domain deals with the basic vocabulary of computer system components. Just how extensive this knowledge should be depends upon the social role of the learner.
3. IMPACT. This domain encompasses the social effects of computerization, including both the positive and negative impacts

of computers on society.

4. LIMITATIONS. This domain is distinguished from the applications domain because of the focus on developing a general sense of the capabilities and limitations of computing machines. Examples of computer limitations include the facts that computers do not have feelings and consciousness, nor are they able to make value judgments.

5. PROGRAMMING/ALGORITHMS. This domain deals with the ability to read, modify, and construct algorithms and programs.

6. SOFTWARE AND DATA PROCESSING. This area includes vocabulary relevant to software, information processing, and data.

7. USAGE. While the foregoing areas are largely cognitive in emphasis, this domain involves motor skills for sequencing and execution of certain tasks on the computer or computer terminal.

8. VALUES AND FEELINGS. The effective domain centers on developing positive attitudes toward personal use of computers as well as balanced attitudes toward computers as a social force.

For the cognitive objectives, the first digit after the letter refers to a cognitive level—1 indicates a low level, generally a skill or knowledge of facts; 2 indicates a higher level of understanding, requiring some analysis and/or synthesis. The final digit is merely a count of items within each level, in some sort of logical sequence. For the psychomotor and affective objectives, the first digit is merely for recording purposes—no attempt was made to suggest any priorities.

The detailed objectives within each of the eight categories follow.

APPLICATIONS (A)

A.1.1.   Recognize that computers and computer-supported applications are used in a wide variety of ways to assist individuals, groups, and institutions.

A.1.2.   Recognize specific uses of computers or computer-supported applications in many of the following areas:
   a.   medicine and health care
   b.   law enforcement and criminal justice
   c.   education and training

31

      d.   engineering and design

      e.   business and banking

      f.   the office

      g.   transportation and traffic control

      h.   defense systems

      i.   weather prediction

      j.   recreation

      k.   government and politics

      l.   the home

      m. the library

      n.   manufacturing

      o.   the creative arts

      p.   publishing

      q.   public utilities—telephone and power plants.

A.1.3.   Recognize that the following are common types of computer applications, and be able to give an example of each type:

      a.   information storage and retrieval—recordkeeping, data bases, etc.

      b.   simulation and modeling

      c.   process/machine control—robotics

      d.   computation (numerical/statistical analysis of data)

      e.   data processing

      f.   word processing

      g.   graphics

      h.   speech synthesis

      i.   artificial intelligence.

A.1.4.   Recognize the definition of and some advantages of computer simulation

A.1.5.   Recognize that computers are generally useful for information-processing tasks which require any of the following:

      a.   handling large amounts of information

      b.   rapid handling of information

      c.   accuracy

      d.   repetition

      e.   storage of information in an accessible form.

A.1.6.   Recognize that some of the more important factors which limit and/or restrict computer use include:

      a.   cost (hardware, software, maintenance, conversion, etc.)

      b.   people's attitudes (fears, anxieties)

      c.   unavailability of suitable software/applications

      d.   hardware limitations—storage limitations, lack of peripherals, etc.

e. complexity of some computer-supported applications.

A.1.7. Recognize that innovations in computer hardware and software continually expand the potential utility of the computer.

A.1.8. Identify some of the features of a computer-supported application which make it easy to use.

A.1.9. Recognize some advantages of using a computer for storage and retrieval of information (including continual updating and quick recall).

A.1.10. Recognize features and capabilities of personal microcomputer systems as compared to features and capabilities of large data processing systems.

A.2.1. Determine how computers and computer-supported applications can assist an individual as he/she plays various roles, i.e., consumer, worker, citizen; how such systems assist groups and organizations as they attempt to accomplish tasks and responsibilities.

A.2.2. Assess the feasibility, potential benefits, and hazards of a computer-supported application (cross-reference in impact).

A.2.3. Design and develop a computer-supported application that would be personally useful.

A.2.4. Recognize some general criteria for computer usage for a particular task (e.g., purpose, time and resource constraints, ethical or moral considerations, relevance).

HARDWARE (H)

H.1.1. Recognize that computer hardware refers to the physical components of computer systems.

H.1.2 Recognize that chips are small pieces of silicon that contain electronic logic networks called circuits, and that a computer can be made up of chips mounted on boards.

H.1.3. Identify at least five major functions of a general purpose computer system, namely input, output, storage or memory, control, arithmetic, and timing or clocking.

H.1.4. Recognize that CPU stands for Central Processing Unit, which is the part of the computer which carries out the essential and controlling tasks. The arithmetic, control, and memory units of a computer are generally regarded as comprising the CPU.

H.1.5. Recognize that the term "mainframe" refers to the CPU and its enclosure or to large computers.

H.1.6. Recognize that a microprocessor is a single chip containing all the electronic logic of a CPU.

H.1.7. Recognize that a microcomputer is a very small computer that uses a microprocessor for its Central Processing Unit.

H.1.8. Recognize that minicomputers are a range of computers larger than microcomputers and smaller than what is usually called "mainframes."

H.1.9. Identify the meaning of acronyms including ROM, RAM, PROM, EPROM, which identify different types of memory.

H.1.10. Recognize the characteristics of secondary storage systems including magnetic tapes, floppy disks, etc.

H.1.11. Recognize that keyboards, punchcards, tapes serve as input devices.

H.1.12. Recognize that display screens, printers, punchcards, tapes serve as output devices.

H.1.13. Recognize the function of some basic communications technology, e.g., networks, distributed networks, modem or acoustic-coupler.

H.1.14. Distinguish parallel and serial communications.

H.1.15. Recognize the rapid growth of computer hardware since the 1940's.

H.1.16. Recognize the distinctions among the following terms: bit, byte, register, and word.

H.1.17. Recognize both the loose and the precise definition of "K."

H.1.18. Distinguish and be able to identify special purpose from general purpose computers.

H.1.19. Identify similarities and differences between programmable calculators and computers.

H.1.20. Distinguish analog and digital computing operations.

IMPACT (I)

I.1.1. Describe some of the more common computer-related careers such as computer programmer, systems analyst, computer scientist, computer operator, key operator.

I.1.2. Recognize that computers and computer-supported applications have a major impact on the way ordinary citizens live, work, and play.

I.1.3. Recognize that for at least the short-term future, computers will continue to be made smaller while the amount of information they can hold will continue to increase.

I.1.4. Recognize that computers are used to commit a variety of serious crimes, especially stealing money and stealing information.

I.1.5. Recognize that identification codes (numbers) and passwords are a primary means for restricting use of computer systems, of computer programs, and of data files.

I.1.6.   Recognize that procedures for detecting computer-based crimes are limited.

I.1.7.   Identify some advantages or disadvantages of a data base containing personal information on a large number of people (the list might include value for research and potential for privacy invasion).

I.1.8.   Recognize several regulatory procedures (e.g., privilege to review one's own file and restrictions on use of universal personal identifiers) which help ensure the integrity of personal data files.

I.1.9.   Recognize that "privacy problems" are characteristic of large information files whether or not they are computerized.

I.1.10. Recognize that computerization both increases and decreases employment.

I.1.11. Recognize that computerization can personalize and impersonalize procedures in fields such as education.

I.1.12. Recognize that computerization can lead to both greater independence and dependence upon one's tools.

I.1.13. Recognize that alleged "computer mistakes" are usually mistakes made by people.

I.2.1.   Plan a strategy for tracing and correcting a computer-related error such as a billing error.

I.2.2.   Explain how computers make keeping track of people more feasible.

I.2.3.   Recognize that even though a person does not go near a computer, he or she is affected indirectly because the society is influenced by computerization.

I.2.4.   Explain how computers can be used to impact the distribution and use of economic, social, and political power.

I.2.5.   Identify and evaluate the positive and negative consequences of computer use in specific situations.

LIMITATIONS (L)

L.1.1.   Recognize that computers are machines designed, built, and operated by humans to assist in many tasks.

L.1.2.   Recognize that computers cannot make value judgments.

L.1.3.   Recognize that computers cannot provide answers to every question.

L.1.4.   Recognize that despite "artificial intelligence," computers cannot think in the way that the word "think" is normally used.

L.1.5. Identify a number of things that computers cannot do or cannot perform efficiently.

L.2.1. Distinguish major differences between human capabilities and computer capabilities.

PROGRAMMING/ALGORITHMS (P)

P.1.1. Recognize the definition of algorithm and that flowcharts and programs are alternative forms for expressing algorithms.

P.1.2. Follow and give the correct output for simple algorithms expressed in words, flowcharts, or structure diagrams. The algorithms would include some or all of the following: replacement; calculation; selection (decision points); repetition (simple looping with iteration/recursion); input and output operations.

P.1.3. Given a simple algorithm, explain what it accomplishes, i.e., be able to interpret and to generalize. As in P.1.2. the algorithm could include replacement, calculation, selection, repetition, and input/output.

P.1.4. For simple programs written in a language such as BASIC or PASCAL, follow and give the correct output for the program. The programs would contain input/output, replacement, calculation, selection, and repetition.

P.2.1. Modify a simple algorithm or program to accomplish a new, but related, task. This would include changing one or two statements to solve a similar problem, and adding more statements to accommodate additional requirements.

P.2.2. Detect syntax and logic errors in an improperly functioning algorithm or program.

P.2.3. Correct syntax and logic errors in an improperly functioning algorithm or program.

P.2.4. Develop, with appropriate documentation, an algorithm or program for solving a specific problem.

P.2.5. Select an appropriate algorithm from a set of alternatives using criteria such as efficiency, elegance, and appropriateness.

SOFTWARE AND DATA PROCESSING (S)

S.1.1. Identify that software refers to computer programs and includes operating systems, compilers, and user (application) programs.

S.1.2. Recognize that digital computers operate upon information which has been encoded in binary, the coding system which can utilize the base 2 number system.

S.1.3. Recognize that a computer needs instructions to operate.

S.1.4. Recognize that a computer gets instructions from a program written in a programming language by a person.

S.1.5. Recognize that computer programs are sets of sequential instructions which perform many tasks such as printing, sorting, calculating.

S.1.6. Identify that the basic elements of an information processing system are input, processing, and output, in that order.

S.1.7. Identify the fact that data are symbols representing things.

S.1.8. Identify the fact that information is data which have been given meaning.

S.1.9. Identify the fact that communication is the transmission of information via coded messages.

S.1.10. Identify the need for data to be organized in order to be useful.

S.1.11. Identify the fact that data processing involves the transformation of data by means of a set of predefined rules.

S.1.12. Recognize that computers process data by searching, sorting, deleting, updating, summarizing, moving.

S.1.13. Recognize that software refers to any nonpermanent sets of programs, whereas firmware refers to software that has been made physically permanent.

S.1.14. Recognize that an operating system is software or firmware that performs file managing tasks such as loading programs, copying files.

S.2.1. Select an appropriate attribute for ordering of data for a particular task.

S.2.2. Design an elementary data structure for a given application (that is, provide order for the data).

S.2.3. Design an elementary coding system for a given application.

USAGE (U)

U.1.1. Connect a microcomputer or computer terminal to a power source and available storage units such as disks or tapes.

U.1.2. Interact with a computer in an online instructional learning situation involving drill and dialogues.

U.1.3. Use system commands for an available computer system (e.g., command to load, list, execute, save, and purge files).

U.1.4. Use program documentation to select and run library programs for specific tasks.

U.1.5. Enter, compile, and debug a simple stored program written in a "higher-level" language.

VALUES (V)

V.1.1. Does not feel fear, anxiety, or intimidation from computer experiences.

V.1.2. Feels confident about his/her ability to use and control computers.

V.1.3. Enjoys and desires work or play with computers, especially computer-assisted learning.

V.1.4. Describes past experiences with computers with positive-affect words like fun, exicting, challenging.

V.1.5. Given an opportunity, spends free time using a computer.

V.1.6. Values the potential role of computers in meeting societal and institutional needs (e.g., making full, accurate information available for relevant decisions, problem solutions, or inquiries by private individuals; handling routine data collection/processing/monitoring tasks efficiently).

V.1.7. Values efficient information processing provided that it does not neglect accuracy, the protection of individual rights, and social needs.

V.1.8. Values computerization of routine tasks so long as it frees people to engage in other activities and is not done as an end in itself.

V.1.9. Values increased communication and availability of information made possible through computer use provided that it does not violate personal rights to privacy and accuracy of personal data.

These objectives have been used as the basis for the development of an assessment instrument designed to measure computer awareness, knowledge, and attitudes among secondary school students. In addition, they have provided a foundation for the development of instructional materials designed to foster computer literacy. Information concerning both these projects is available from the Minnesota Educational Computing Consortium, 2520 Broadway Drive, St. Paul, MN 55113.

CONCLUSION

The growing reliance of our society upon computer systems demands that the public come to understand this phenomenon. Our schools are charged with the responsibility to develop instructional programs in computer literacy, which is generally understood to refer to the level of knowledge and skill a person needs to function effectively in a computerized society. Although not everyone agrees on what that knowledge consists of, it is possible to define the major components or dimensions of computer literacy. We have attempted to provide information concerning computer literacy which will be helpful to educators preparing or complementing instruction designed to promote computer awareness and understanding. In keeping with this objective, we conclude with a rather extensive list of references.

References

1. Amara, R. *Toward Understanding the Social Impact of Computers.* Menlo Park, Calif.: Institute for the Future, 1974.

2. Anderson, Ronald E. "National Computer Literacy, 1980." Paper presented at the National Computer Literacy Goals for 1985 Conference, December 18, 1980.

3. Anderson, Ronald E., and Klassen, Daniel L. "A Conceptual Framework for Developing Computer Literacy Instruction." *AEDS Journal* 14, no. 3 (1981): 128–50.

4. ——; Krohn, Karl; and Sandman, Richard. *User Guide for the Minnesota Computer Literacy and Awareness Assessment.* St. Paul: Minnesota Educational Computing Consortium, 1980.

5. ——; Hansen, T.P.; Johnson, D.C.; and Klassen, D.L. "Minnesota Computer Literacy and Awareness Assessment, Form 8." St. Paul: Minnesota Educational Computing Consortium, 1979.

6. ——; ——; ——; and ——. "Instructional Computing: Acceptance and Rejection by Secondary School Teachers." *Sociology of Work and Occupation* 6, no. 2 (1979): 227–50.

7. ——; Klassen, Daniel; Hansen, Thomas P.; and Johnson, David C. "The Affective and Cognitive Effects of Microcomputer-Based Science Instruction." *Journal of Educational Technology Systems* (Spring 1981).

8. Austing, R.H.; Barnes, B.H.; Bonnette, D.T.; Engel, G.L.; and Stokes, G. "Curriculum '78: Recommendations for the Undergraduate Program in Computer Science." *Communications of the ACM* 22, no. 3 (1979): 147–65.

9. ——; and Engel, G.L. "Recent Developments in Computers and Society Research and Education." *Proceedings of the National Computer Conference, 1979;* pp. 407–410.

10. Ball, M., and Charp, S. *Be a Computer Literate.* Morristown, N.J.: Creative Computing Press, 1977.

11. Bell, D. *The Coming of the Post-Industrial Society.* New York: Basic Books, 1973.

12. Bell, F.H. "Computer Literacy, School Mathematics, and Problem

Solving: Three for the Price of One." *AEDS Journal* 12, no. 4 (1977): 163–70.

13. Billings, K., and Moursund, D. *Are You Computer Literate?* Forest Grove, Ore.: Dilithium Press, 1979.

14. Carpenter, Thomas P., et. al. "The Current Status of Computer Literacy: NAEP Results for Secondary Students." *Mathematics Teacher* (December 1980): 669–73.

15. "The Computer Society." *TIME*, February 20, 1978.

16. "Computers in Higher Education, Report to the President's Science Advisory Committee." Washington, D.C., 1967; and "CERI-Report Extracts," *International World of Computer Education*, vol. 1, no. 5, 1974.

17. Conference Board of the Mathematical Sciences. *Recommendations Regarding Computers in High School Education*. Washington, D.C.: Conference Board, 1972.

18. Denenberg, S.A. "An Alternative Curriculum for Computer Literacy Development." *AEDS Journal* 13, no. 2 (1980): 156.

19. Dennis, J.R. "Training Preservice Teachers to Teach with Computers." *AEDS Journal* 11, no. 2 (1978): 25–30.

20. Friel, S., and Roberts, N. "Computer Literacy Bibliography." *Creative Computing* 6, no. 9 (1980): 92–97.

21. Hansen, T.P.; Klassen, D.L.; Anderson, R.E.; and Johnson, D.C. "Computer Literacy Courses." *AEDS Monitor* 18, no. 5 (1979): 29–30.

22. Holzman, T.G., and Glaser, R. "Developing Computer Literacy in Children: Some Observations and Suggestions." *Educational Technology* (August 1977): 5–11.

23. Hopper, J.A. "A Byte of Basic." *Proceedings of National Educational Computing Conference, 1980*, Norfolk, Va., pp. 62–64.

24. Hunter, B.C. *An Approach to Integrating Computer Literacy into the K–8 Curriculum*. Alexandria, Va.: Human Resources Research Organization, 1980.

25. ——. *Successful Programs in Computer Literacy*. Alexandria, Va.: Human Resources Research Organization, 1977.

26. Johnson, D.C.; Anderson, R.E.; Hansen, T.P.; and Klassen, D.L. "Computer Literacy—What Is It?" *Mathematics Teacher* 73, (1980): 91–96.

27. Klassen, D.L.; Anderson, R.E.; Hansen, T.P.; and Johnson, D.C. *A Study of Computer Use and Literacy in Science Education, Final Report*. St. Paul: Minnesota Educational Computing Consortium, 1980.

28. Kurshan, B. *Computer Literacy: Practical Ways to Teach the Basic Mathematical Skills*. Richmond, Va.: Virginia Council of Teachers of Mathematics, 1978.

29. Longworth, N.A. "A Course on 'Information' for the Secondary School." In *Computers in Education*, edited by O. Lecarme and R.

Lewis, pp. 749–54. Amsterdam: North Holland Publishing Co., 1975.

30. Luehrmann, Arthur. "Computer Literacy—What Should It Be?" *Mathematics Teacher* 74, no. 9 (1981): 682–86.

31. ———. "Computer Literacy—A National Crisis and a Solution for It." *BYTE* 5, no. 7 (1980): 98–102, 167–70.

32. ———. "Should the Computer Teach the Student, or Vice Versa?" *Creative Computing* 2, no. 6 (1976): 42–45.

33. Lykos, P.G. "The Computer Illiteracy Problem: A Partial Solution." *American Mathematical Monthly* 81, no. 4 (1974): 393–98.

34. Makkar, L. "Computer Awareness for All, or If They Are All Right, What's Wrong?" *Computer Education* 15 (1973): 21–22.

35. Michael, E.N. "The Unprepared Society." New York: Basic Books, 1968.

36. Molnar, Andrew R. "The Coming of Computer Literacy: Are We Prepared for It?" *Educational Technology* (January 1981): 26–28.

37. ———. "The Next Great Crisis in American Education: Computer Literacy." *Journal: Technological Horizons in Education* 5, no. 4 (July/August 1978): 35–39.

38. Moursund, D. *Basic Programming for Computer Literacy.* New York: McGraw-Hill, 1978.

39. ———. "Microcomputers Will Not Solve the Computers-in-Education Problem." *AEDS Journal* 13, no. 1 (1979): 31–39.

40. ———. "Selecting Goals for an Introductory Computer Programming Course." *Mathematics Teacher* (1973): 599–603.

41. ———. "What Is Computer Literacy?" *Creative Computing* 2, no. 6 (1976): 55.

42. National Council of Teachers of Mathematics. *An Agenda for Action: Recommendations for School Mathematics of the 1980's.* Reston, Va.: The Council, 1980.

43. Neill, M.J. "An Empirical Method of Identifying Instructional Objectives for a High School Computer Literacy Curriculum." Doctoral dissertation, University of Oregon, 1977.

44. Pella, M.O.; O'Hearn, G.T.; Gale, C.W. "Referents to Scientific Literacy." *Journal of Research in Science Teaching* 4 (1966): 199–208.

45. Porat, Marc Uri. *The Information Economy.* Washington, D.C.: Department of Commerce, Office of Telecommunications and the National Science Foundation. Government Printing Office, 1977.

46. Press, L.I. "Towards General Information Processing Literacy." *Proceedings of CCUC/5, 1974,* pp. 325–29.

47. Rawitsch, D.G. "The Concept of Computer Literacy." *MAEDS Journal of Educational Computing* 2, no. 2 (1978): 1–19.

48. Schiming, B.B. "A Case for Information Literacy." *Proceedings of NECC/2,* pp. 58–61. National Educational Computing Conference, 1980.

49. Stevens, D.J. "How Educators Perceive Computers in the Class-

room." *AEDS Journal* 13, no. 3 (1980): 221–31.

50. Taylor, R.P. "Computing Competencies for Teachers—A Preliminary Protection for All But the Teacher of Computing." *Proceedings of National Educational Computing Conference, 1980.*

51. Thomas, R.A. "Computer Literacy in the High School." *AEDS Journal* 9, no. 3 (1976): 71–77.

52. Turkle, S. "Computer as Rorschach." *Society* 17, no. 2 (1980): 15–24.

53. Watt, D.H. *Computer Literacy: What Schools Should Be Doing About It.* Cambridge, Mass.: Artificial Intelligence Laboratory, Massachusetts Institute of Technology, 1980.

54. Wexler, H. "Computer Literacy—Research Developments." *American Education* 15 (1979): 41–42.

3. Computertown, U.S.A.

Bob Albrecht, Louise Burton, and Ramon Zamora

COMPUTERTOWN CENTER—THE LIBRARY

A dot flashes in the center of an unidentified state map. The computer waits. The name of the state is . . . ? The nine-year-old at the keyboard wiggles, then turns questioningly to her mother. "Well," mom says, "where did Dorothy live in *The Wizard of Oz*?"

"Kansas! Kansas!" Enlightenment. The child types the word and hits ENTER. The flashing dot moves to another state. This time, the child knows the state and quickly responds to the computer's query. Gaining confidence, she follows the flashing dot, naming state after state with occasional help from her mother. A crowd of kibitzers gathers behind her to share in this computer game.

Across the room, children are arguing about whether to buy silk or arms. They are playing TAIPAN, a well-researched simulation of the seagoing China trade in the middle 1800's. They receive a great deal of unsolicited advice from others waiting their turn to play the game.

Elsewhere in the room, very young children are intrigued by simple math and verbal games. Older children are exploring labyrinths, trying to color a map using only four colors, developing strategies for beating the computer at MAXIT! an elegant game of positive and negative numbers.

The most intense group is clustered about Swordquest, a fantasy game of exploration and problem solving. They don't know it, but they are teaching themselves intuitive probability, contingency planning, resource conservation, and, especially, how to use information.

It is Tuesday evening in Menlo Park, California, and the place is the public library. Every Tuesday evening, the Dragons of Menlo Park (sometimes known as the editors of *Recreational Computing Magazine*) bring computers to the library. After the first such event in March 1979, the sessions were mobbed. Children greatly outnumber adults at the library gatherings, and those with several weeks' experience teach their friends.

There are many more children than computers. So, while waiting to play with computers, children wander about the library, and discover—the library! Books, magazines, tapes, records, educational toys—all are there to play with and learn from. Children who had never been to the library now come regularly, lured by computers, then enchanted by the wonders of a public place dedicated to helping people learn.

What is happening in Computertown, U.S.A. can happen in any school resource center, media center, library, learning center—or whatever it may be called.

The parents sense that something special is happening. They want to learn too! Increasingly, children and parents work together to learn about computers and, through computers, learn other things.

Enter Commodore! One Tuesday evening, Larry Perry, Director of Marketing for Commodore Business Machines, wandered into Computertown, U.S.A. Since he happened to have a PET computer under his arm, he was cheerfully welcomed by dozens of children. At 9 P.M., Larry left, but the PET stayed, on loan to the library.

The arrival of a full-time PET signaled the next phase of Computertown, U.S.A. The Dragons, always ready to play with children, started very short, one-hour courses to teach children how to use the PET computer. By the end of the summer of 1979, more than 300 7- to 13-year-olds had learned to use the PET. During the next few months, every 7- to 13-year-old in Menlo Park had the opportunity to learn how to use a computer. Where? In Computertown Center, the Menlo Park Library.

By the fall of 1981, the library acquired four additional PETs. All five, located in the Children's Section, are in constant use, from the moment the library opens until closing time. At dinnertime, librarians are besieged with phone calls from parents, asking that children be sent home for more conventional nourishment.

Coming soon are more computers. A Radio Shack TRS-80 is on the way. An Apple computer is available, waiting for a color TV. Expectations are high that several more computers will be acquired during the 1981-82 school year.

As for software, hundreds of programs are available for educational and recreational use—games, simulations, drill and practice. A wide selection will be available in the library.

Soon we will begin preparing teach-yourself-style instructional materials so that 7- to 13-year-olds can teach themselves how to program the library computers. These materials will emphasize verbal activities, graphics, music, games, and math recreations.

And that is only the beginning of the story.

KEPLER'S BOOKSTORE

A humanities professor sits down at a computer and threads his way past the monsters in a dungeon. Strange, very strange, he keeps thinking. He had simply wandered into one of his regular literary hangouts and found a group of people playing with computers. Now he was trying it. It is Friday night in Menlo Park, and the place is Kepler's Bookstore.

On the third Friday of every month, people bring computers to Kepler's, a large down-home bookstore, with a section of tables and chairs, catering to browsers and good conversation. The bottomless coffee pot encourages people to relax, think, talk, and enjoy. Families come to Kepler's.

Once a month, the media of yesterday and today (books) mingle with the media of the future (books and computers). People who come to Kepler's to browse among stacks of books can also browse among piles of cassettes—cassettes that play through computers.

As always with computers, children plunge into the keyboards while adults are content to watch. But more and more, as computer anxiety lessens, parents are willing to learn with their children. This is serendipity.

ROUND TABLE PIZZA

Monday night is the Smiths' night out, and by family vote, dinner is pizza. What do they discover when they arrive at their local pizza parlor? Several picnic tables given over to computers. And where is it happening? Why, Menlo Park, of course.

On the fourth Monday of every month, people bring computers to the Round Table Pizza in Menlo Park. A common complaint is "Suzie, your pizza is getting cold." Suzie, of course, is engrossed in playing TAIPAN or MAXIT! or WHAT STATE AM I? or some other computer game. Eventually, a parent comes to retrieve Suzie, and then mother's pizza gets cold as she and Suzie play and learn together.

Perhaps you have been to pizza parlors, bars, taverns, and other places, in which arcade games gobble up quarters. We are not talking about that kind of game. In Computertown, U.S.A., children play games that demand the highest level of thought—analysis of information, careful consideration of how to use the information, and application of processes based upon the analysis—in other words, the highest form of problem solving. And—it's fun!

Perhaps the most amazing thing occurs when a teacher, who happens to be at the Round Table, watches his or her student *gladly and joyously* learn, in a few minutes, something the teacher has tried to *teach* for a year. Is there an "Inner Game of Learning"?

THE ULTIMATE LEARNING CENTER

Computertown, U.S.A. is a small city of 27,000 people. The entire community is becoming a learning center for the people who live here—children and adults. Soon, we will ask the elders to help. Menlo Park has an unusually large population of elders, many of whom have been teachers.

This can be a new coalition, of elders who thought they had retired and children who want to learn. The place? Public places—libraries, pizza parlors, bookstores, parks, community centers. Even schools— if they choose to participate.

Where? Everywhere. Computertown, U.S.A. is any town in which parents, children, elders work together to build a place in which everyone can learn. In Computertown, U.S.A., we use computers to do those things that computers do well. People do those things that people do well.

The ultimate learning center is a state of mind, a way of doing things. Computertown, U.S.A. is a place in which we begin with computers, but include everything, in a learning center for those who live here.

WHAT NEXT?

Soon, most children in Menlo Park will know how to use and enjoy computers. Already, they are asking for more. Adults also want to learn more. Here are some things we are doing:

- A series of courses called "Computers for Kids and Parents." These courses, conducted through a nearby community college, require 7- to 13-year-olds and a parent to enroll as a team to learn how to use, program, and enjoy home computers.
- Courses and workshops for adults, covering more "serious" uses of computers.
- Workshops for teachers who wish to learn (1) how to run their own field trips at the library and (2) how to use computers in a classroom setting.
- A Master Class for children who wish to learn to program in good programming style and to completely and properly docu-

ment their programs. They will also learn to criticize and evaluate professionally written programs and be encouraged to submit articles to computer and educational periodicals.

Is the message clear? Computertown, U.S.A. is for everyone—children, parents, elders, teachers. Everyone works together to learn whatever is worthwhile learning. We can do it—everyone can do it—and computers will help.

4. Computer Games: An Educational Tool Beyond Compare

David H. Ahl

It's 1847. Your team of oxen has been pulling your wagon across Kansas for the last two weeks and you figure you've been covering a good fifteen miles a day. At the Republican River you decide to ford it and find it deeper than you thought. The wagon is swamped and you lose most of your food and clothes. Fortunately you had secured your medical supplies and ammunition high in the wagon and didn't lose those too. But now you have to decide whether to make for the next fort, which is three days away, or to stop and hunt. Since you're in buffalo country, you decide to hunt and wait until later to stop at the fort.

And so it continues in the computer game Oregon Trail. During your six-month journey you face attacks from wild animals, Indians, and bandits. Your wagon can be swamped, break a wheel, or even have a fire. Your oxen can be injured or wander off. In the mountains, heavy rains, snow, and impassable trails are constant hazards. Illness and injuries are always a threat.

Fewer than 30 per cent of the pioneers who set off from Independence, Missouri, from 1840 to 1870 ever made it to the west coast. Now it's your turn to see if you can be one of the survivors. But at least if you don't survive, you have another chance.

How would you like to learn about history by living it through a computer game? Given the choice, millions of students are opting for the computer game and their teachers are finding that the lessons are better learned than those provided by the traditional textbook.

These types of games, sometimes called simulations, are available in many subject areas for many grade levels. In social studies, for example, using the program Hammurabi, young children can learn how a simple economic system works. Players decide how much grain to plant each year, how much to feed their people, and how much to buy or sell from neighboring city-states. Harvests are good in some years, bad in others. And sometimes rats get into the grain bins. King, a more complex simulation in the same vein, introduces the problems of industrial development, pollution, and tourism. Students can experience economics on a local scale with Lemonade Stand. In this program, players must decide how much lemonade to make, how much to charge, and how many signs to make. An outside variable is the weather; rainy days are not good for lemonade sales. On the other hand, circus parades are good for sales.

Science and ecology simulations allow players to experience situations and experiment with variables that are far beyond the reach of any normal classroom or textbook. In Malaria, for example, students must try to control a malaria outbreak in a Central American country. Pesticides, treatment for the ill, preventive inoculations, and field hospitals are the variables to be controlled. Students discover that if cost is no object, the disease is easy to control; but unfortunately in most tropical countries, cost is a major obstacle. Tag lets students experiment with the tagging-and-recovery method of measuring wildlife populations. Users of Sterl try to control the destructive screw worm fly with various types of pesticides as well as male sterilization.

In English, games such as Hangman and Don't Fall help teach children word skills in a highly motivational way. The program in Madlibs and Red Riding creates funny, often hilarious, stories. For stories to be readable, however, the player must use various parts of speech correctly. Spelling, Haiku, Bard, and other games provide practice in other aspects of language arts.

Adventure is a widely popular computer game in which players explore a Tolkien-like environment complete with trolls, animals, treasures, and a landscape of hills, ravines, forests, and caves. Players give the computer commands such as "Go West," Pick Up Lamp," or "Drink Water." The object is (1) to discover how to play the game; and (2) to overcome the obstacles, find the treasures, and return to "civilization." Imagine playing this fascinating and addictive game in French! Or Spanish. Or German. Language teachers have never had such a powerful motivational tool with which to teach. It's like parachuting the student into the middle of a foreign country with the instructions: "Learn to speak the language and you will be able to survive, find some treasure, and escape."

Similarly fascinating games have been produced in other subject areas: mathematics, geometry, and logic (where they all started), physics, chemistry, biology, economics, business, medicine, geology, and many others.

Computer games know no age limits. For the Sesame Place theme parks, Creative Computing Software has developed a series of games for players who cannot yet read. At the Lighthouse School in Wisconsin, first to third graders write their own games. Elementary and secondary schools, colleges, and graduate schools throughout the United States use games. In Salt Lake City, a public education center teaches adults English language skills via computer, while several museums have computer game exhibits oriented to visitors of all ages.

Computers were not invented to play games. But, from the very beginning, computerists found that these machines can be programmed to play games—extremely well. Additionally, the known motivation of games and the fact that computer games tend to increase personal interaction and peer tutoring make computer games one of the most powerful educational tools currently available.

Are your students using computer games? If they are not, they ought to be—today!

5. The Computer and Exceptional Children

Henry S. Kepner, Jr.

The computer has the capability to assist in the education of students with identifiable physical or intellectual handicaps as well as in the education of students identified as gifted. For these students, the computer has unique strengths that help them function in an enriched environment. For example, deaf students in a nationwide pilot project can communicate instantaneously with each other using a computer over telephone lines. For students with learning difficulties, the computer is a nonjudgmental interactive tutor or drillmaster that repeats items as long as the student requests repetition. For gifted students, the computer is a self-contained world with a given set of vocabulary and syntax to be explored. In attempting to control the computer, the gifted student accepts a major challenge.

PHYSICAL HANDICAPS

The computer is being adapted to help individuals with a variety of physical handicaps. Since the computer is capable of controlling machinery, this use should be no surprise. Through computer terminals deaf individuals can now converse with people far away. In this mode, the written word, as seen on paper or television monitor, is the vehicle for communication (4). With the improvement of voice synthesizers, the computer is becoming a communication aid for the blind. Written communication, stored on the computer, can be sounded out by the computer and its voice synthesizer. Using a set of grammatical rules to sound out words, the voice simulates human speech. If the rules fail, the student can order the computer to spell the word with the voice synthesizer used in the Speak and Spell educational device (3). Major improvements in optical scanners have made it possible for the blind to read any book instantly. Instead of a typist first entering the words in a computer, a scanner picks up the letters directly from the page. This device works like the optical scanners in grocery and department stores that pick up inventory codes and prices. Using the scanner and voice synthesizer under computer control, the blind individual can read any typed information unassisted by other people.

Individuals with speech defects can now communicate clearly with others through the computer. They have the option of using a computer printout which prints their typed message on paper or on a portable video screen, or of using a voice synthesizer to present their message orally.

For hearing-impaired students with speech defects, a new instructional technique is being explored. A word is spoken correctly and an electronic image of the sound produced is displayed graphically on the video screen. The hearing-impaired student says the same word and compares his or her voice image with the original image. In trying to make the two images match, the student may gain control over his or her speech mechanism.

For individuals who lack motor control or who are without limbs, the computer can control part of their environment. By means of typed messages, the computer can control objects they cannot otherwise control such as motorized wheelchairs, special telephones, home appliances. For many handicapped students, the microprocessor has given them access to the world outside their private room or home.

INTELLECTUAL HANDICAPS

For students with a variety of intellectual handicaps, the computer can provide special assistance and practice as needed. For example, Pollard reports the use of a microcomputer to help a 10-year-old with dyslexia perform "rote learning of simple basic words" (2, p. 9).

The computer can be a welcome taskmaster to students who have felt the frustration and disapproval of adults or peers in their endless attempts to master a specific set of math facts, words, or sounds. It can be programmed to present tasks repeatedly in the same format without showing emotion. Thus, the child's eagerness to succeed is satisfied by success and not dampened by external disapproval.

The use of a computer allows a student to succeed even though the way of mastering and the rate of learning differ significantly from typical teacher expectations. Student performance levels can be recorded, and the teacher can monitor student progress without being involved in the drill activity.

Cook summarized the advantages of a computerized instructional system for an exceptional child's needs as follows:

1. Active learning with high student response rate

2. Immediate feedback and reinforcement
3. Maintenance of attention
4. Individual pacing of instruction
5. Infinite patience with sufficient repetition to insure learning. (1, p. 7)

Although specific instructional programs are just becoming available, the reader should be on the lookout for materials to be tested for exceptional students.

GIFTED AND TALENTED CHILDREN

Despite a small quantity of literature on the use of computers with gifted and talented students, such use is widespread. Without formal courses, these students accept the challenge of the computer as an environment to be explored and mastered. The natural curiosity expressed by "How did it do that?" can be heard repeatedly as students watch and then try things with a computer.

To talented students, the microcomputer presents a self-contained, harmless environment waiting to be controlled. The adult must be sure to stay out of the way and not hinder the students' ability to explore independently. The major responsibility of the teacher is to pose appropriate problems for students to tackle. There are varied sources of good computer challenge problems—for example, the magazine *Creative Computing.*

The psychology used in this context is different from that used in most classroom settings. The teacher must have the confidence to present an area to be explored and stay out of the way of student problem solving. With great pride, the author can report that he has always learned new things about the computer *from his students* when he has not put limits on their explorations. It is important that the teacher not let his or her ego inhibit student activity.

The author has worked with high school students, intermediate grade students, and middle school students in this open-ended mode with excellent results. Unfortunately, many students report that this computer work is one of the few school activities they have experienced where they were not forced to follow a set sequence of instruction and drill—even if they did not need the drill.

References

1. Cook, C., et al. *OCCE Special Report: Computers in Special Education.* Eugene, Ore.: Oregon Council for Computer Education, Department of Computer Science, University of Oregon, 1975.

2. Pollard, J. "Testimony to a Micro—Peter Can Now Read." *Recreational Computing*, 7, no. 6 (May–June 1979): 8–12.

3. Seyfriend, D. J., and Lowe, D. "Microcomputers in Teaching Handicapped Students." *AEDS Monitor* (November 1980): 14–15.

4. Szwedo, K. "Marie Carole's Unusual Home." *Scholastic SCOPE*, January 24, 1980; p. 18.

5. Taber, Florence M. "The Microcomputer—Its Applicability to Special Education." *Focus on Exceptional Children* 14, no. 2 (October 1981): 1–15.

6. The Microcomputer in the Elementary School

Linda Borry Hausmann and Henry S. Kepner, Jr.

The microcomputer is one of the most exciting new resources available to elementary school teachers. Its sudden appearance in elementary buildings is a result of the accessibility of inexpensive computers and the vision of varied intellectual use by students and teachers. The computer has three major functions in the classroom resource center:

1. It has great potential as an instructional tool in many parts of the curriculum.
2. It provides an environment for students to explore through accepting the challenge to gain mastery over the machine—a fascination seen in part through children's excitement with sophisticated videogames.
3. It has valuable recordkeeping features for the teacher.

This article briefly explores each of these areas of use.

INSTRUCTIONAL TOOL

When the microcomputer is used as an instructional tool, prewritten computer programs, called software, direct student use of the machine. Software for drills, tutorials, simulations, and educational games is becoming available for microcomputers. Let's take a look at each use.

Drills

A substantial portion of the elementary school day is devoted to the development of skills in computation, language arts, and other areas. The computer can be a very effective resource in skill development, particularly through the drill-and-practice programs that are available in many subject areas. In these programs, the teacher does the teaching. The computer's role is to reinforce what has been taught by presenting drills. The computer is a very suitable device for presenting drills because it has infinite patience, it can evaluate a student's progress and present problems at an appropriate level of difficulty, and it can provide instantaneous feedback to the student.

In addition, the graphics and sound capabilities of some microcomputers can be used to make the drill more fun and more attractive to students. A well-designed program can be so motivating that students want to do extra drills.

Drill-and-practice programs can be used in many subject areas—for math facts, language art concepts, geography concepts and skills such as locating states and countries on a map, and even for fundamental music skills and ear training.

The professional commercial market has a tremendous number of drill programs. Many are early attempts to use the computer. Others are increasingly sophisticated programs with special computer features such as graphics, sound, and speed that often enhance the drill setting, rather than just duplicate a teacher-made drill. The Milliken Publishing Company, for example, has produced comprehensive drill programs in mathematics, language arts, and reading (2). Although not perfect, these products lead the way in developing a sequence of drill activities for an elementary curriculum.

Tutorials

In tutorial applications, the computer does the teaching. Tutorials are very appropriate in situations where students need extra review or new and challenging material, or where a teacher is not available. With declining enrollment and budget tightening, some schools are unable to offer as many courses as they would like. Computer-based tutorials offer a way to supplement the curriculum offerings, they have great potential in adult or continuing education, and they can be used at the learner's convenience. A good tutorial presents the material in an interesting and motivating way and provides frequent checks on learners' progress. It also gives learners control over their learning.

At this time, despite the sudden inclusion of microcomputers in schools, very few tutorials are available at the elementary level. These programs are expensive and time-consuming to develop. Thus, more time is needed to write such materials.

Simulations

The elementary school years are a time of exploration for the child. Simulations allow the child to explore concepts through playing such roles as that of a fish trying to survive in a lake, or a young entrepreneur trying to sell lemonade on a summer day, or an explorer trying to reach the new world. The computer does not tell children they are right or wrong. It merely acts on their decisions and

56

lets them know the results. If one strategy does not work, children are free to try another. They learn to evaluate their own decisions and take responsibility for them.

The development of simulations for science and social studies explorations is moving rapidly. Numerous examples have been refined or developed at the Minnesota Educational Computing Consortium (3).

Educational Games

Students love to play computer-based games. The popularity of video games is a known fact; students are willing to spend their own money to play them. Why not take the fun of a video game and incorporate it into an educational setting? Students like to have a goal, they enjoy taking risks, and they thrive on competition when they have a chance of winning. These elements can be worked into the setting of an educational game. Students can thus enjoy competing against the computer or against other students in a game that requires mastery of math facts, or skill in logic or other educational topics.

AN ENVIRONMENT TO EXPLORE

One major purpose of schooling is to prepare students to handle new situations. The computer is a highly structured piece of technology that can be controlled through appropriate communication. In his book, *Mindstorms, Children, Computers, and Powerful Ideas*, Papert states:

> In my vision, *the child programs the computer* and, in so doing, both acquires a sense of mastery over a piece of the most modern and powerful technology and establishes an intimate contact with some of the deepest ideas from science, from mathematics, and from the art of intellectual model building. (65, p. 5)

For student exploration of computers, the areas of computer literacy and problem solving are key factors.

Computer Literacy

As the computer affects more and more facets of our lives, computer literacy for students becomes essential. Students need a basic understanding of how computers work and how they will affect their lives. Since a large proportion of children now in school will be working in careers where they will need to deal with computers, computer instruction in the classroom is important.

During the elementary school years, students should have increased opportunity to use computers for a variety of tasks. They should also have the opportunity to explore elementary programming concepts. These programming techniques should be presented in response to student needs, not as sets of rules with little perceived value.

Problem Solving

The computer is a powerful vehicle for developing problem-solving skills. Its computational capabilities free students to explore strategies for solving problems rather than forcing them to wade through computations. Some students improve their problem-solving skills through learning to program in the BASIC language. A special language called LOGO has been developed specifically to help students develop such skills. This language, which is expected to be very popular in elementary classrooms, is now available for Apple and Texas Instruments microcomputers. It provides a rich setting in which students can experiment with control over the computer through an easy-to-use language and syntax.

Problem solving can take a variety of forms. With minimal direct instruction, elementary students can tackle exciting programming problems. The graphics capabilities of the Apple, PET, and TRS-80 microcomputers provide excellent topics of study. The immediate feedback of computer use places the student in an independent learning situation. And in solving a problem, the student studies computer manuals and talks with other computer users.

RECORDKEEPING

Although student problem solving is the most important reason for microcomputers, the teacher can benefit, too. Many teacher records and repetitive forms can be stored and used on computers.

Computer-Managed Instruction

In most elementary schools, teachers spend several hours each day on recordkeeping activities. Teachers need many of these records for their own decisionmaking and some of them to meet building, district, or state requirements. These recordkeeping needs are particularly burdensome in schools that emphasize individualization. In order to properly group their children, teachers have to know which students have mastered which objectives in each subject. A computer-managed instruction package can assist the teacher in scoring tests, updating information on mastery of objectives, providing individualized student prescriptions, and grouping students. It is not a cure-all for all recordkeeping problems, but it does help the teacher in analyzing data and keeping records.

With student information stored on computers, it can be brought out and sorted for various purposes. Reports to parents, progress on IEP's (individualized education programs), and lesson sequences can be retrieved, for example.

Materials Generation

Teachers enjoy having individualized materials for their students. They can use the computer to generate materials for students based on teacher-determined parameters. For example, teachers can store math objectives and test items on the computer and then have it print tests or worksheets for individual students based on those objectives. Teachers can also use the computer to generate crossword puzzles and wordfind puzzles based on words of their choosing. Such puzzles are fun for students and can reinforce spelling and vocabulary. These computer-generated materials applications require a printer.

SUPPORTING INSTRUCTIONAL COMPUTING IN THE ELEMENTARY SCHOOL

Like any other technological innovation, the microcomputer needs to be correctly implemented and properly supported. Before its arrival in a school, the school must be prepared. The administration must be knowledgeable and ready to support the new acquisition. Some key individual in the school must be trained and ready to help teachers, and manage the microcomputer. A room or location must be selected and prepared. Decisions must be made concerning microcomputer use and scheduling.

Among those schools that have had problems in implementing their microcomputers, one common denominator seems to be that they received the microcomputer before they were ready for it. Frequently, well-meaning district administrators give a microcomputer to each elementary school in a large district, assuming that someone in the school will figure out what to do with it. In such cases, the schools are not ready for the equipment and make poor use of it.

In contrast, many of the schools that have the most successful programs have had to work to get their microcomputers. Some have had school or PTA fundraising events or drives. These schools know what they want, are eager to get it, and make good use of it when it arrives.

In some larger districts, the administration has used an incentive policy. Before a school receives a microcomputer, it must meet certain requirements. These requirements usually involve participation by several teachers from the school in an intensive training on the use of the microcomputer in the classroom. Such incentive policies are generally successful in preparing schools to use the microcomputers.

It is also important to provide training opportunities for as many teachers as possible. The more teachers who know about using the microcomputer, the better the school's program will be. If some type of in-service credit can be granted for the training, teachers are often more willing to spend some of their own time to become knowledgeable in using the new tool.

Once the microcomputer is in the school and things are running smoothly, the need for support does not stop. A wise school administrator budgets time for the school's computer coordinator to work with teachers; to attend meetings; and to participate in local, state, and national conferences dealing with computer use in the classroom. In this fast-changing and exciting field it is important to keep up with whatever is happening. In addition, school media centers should keep recent copies of the many good computer-related books and magazines that are available.

The technology in microcomputers has made computing in the elementary school classroom a reality. Their size, price, ease of use, and friendliness have contributed to their popularity. A wide variety of software is available now, and teachers can expect to see rapid growth in the amount of quality software that will be available to them. The next few years should be exciting ones for educational computing in the elementary school.

References

1. Larsen, Sally Greenwood. *Computers for Kids.* Morristown, N.J.: Creative Computing Press, 1981.
2. Milliken Publishing Co., 1100 Research Blvd., St. Louis, MO 63132.
3. Minnesota Educational Computing Consortium, 2520 Broadway Dr., St. Paul, MN 55113.

4. Moursund, David. *Introduction to Computers in Education for Elementary and Middle School Teachers.* Eugene, Ore.: International Council for Computers in Education, Department of Computer and Information Science, University of Oregon, 1981 ($7.00).
5. Papert, Seymour. *Mindstorms, Children, Computers, and Powerful Ideas.* New York: Basic Books, 1980.

7. The Computer in Language Arts and Reading

Henry S. Kepner, Jr.

The computer has the potential to be an integral part of language and reading instruction. To date, computer use has typically been limited to drill activities in spelling, vocabulary, reading, and grammar. It enhances individualization and performs recordkeeping and prearranged curriculum sequencing.

Beyond these drill capabilities, however, educators are developing expanded uses. On the PLATO system, for example, the computer pictorially acts out a sentence constructed by the student using a limited vocabulary. Recent advances in voice synthesizers have tied voice and print together for early reading activites (8). In addition, word processing is an exciting way to carry out writing tasks.

Two large-scale curriculum drill packages in reading and language arts have been available for several years on specialized large computers. The Computer Curriculum Corporation, using materials initiated at Stanford University, and Control Data Corporation, marketing the PLATO system, have school-tested programs for individualized practice. In these programs, students usually perform drill activities in reading or language arts for about 10 minutes a day. Their performance is monitored by the computer, and the level of difficulty is adjusted based on a prearranged scale and student performance records.

Recently, numerous smaller programs have become available for use on microcomputers. Because of limited machine memory and limited storage on tapes or computer disks, these programs are less comprehensive in curriculum coverage and require more teacher management. Nevertheless, the mobility of, and access to, microcomputers suggest heavy use of these programs in the next few years. One indication of this direction is the recent move of textbook companies into the marketing of computer programs in reading and language arts. After several years of ignoring this form of instruction, most companies acknowledge the need to have materials for computer-assisted drill. A warning to the reader should be sufficient: Evaluate these programs carefully before purchasing them. Many computer programs do not respond well to the student who makes errors. Others may be of little educational value to the student because of poor question sequencing, flashy but unnecessary graphics or sound, incorrect content, or confusing directions or screen format. (See the article "Computer Software in Education.")

On the positive side, the availability of microcomputers has put the experimental tool in the hands of teachers, curriculum developers, professors, and hobbyists. With so many individuals and groups experimenting, exciting uses are developing. A newly released set of 198 English usage exercises—an experimentation with short skill lessons and a set of sentence exercises for ten-minute sessions—is one example (13). These materials are targeted for upper elementary and middle school students. Heuer gives a short description of the innovative process in developing a reading comprehension activity (4). In this setting, a short story is generated on the video screen and followed by multiple choice questions. Teachers can insert their own stories and questions to suit the levels and topics desired.

Major advances in computer graphics and sound promise a full spectrum of capabilities in language development. Touch- or light-sensitive video screens allow the child to point to a location on the screen. The child can identify a picture that corresponds to a printed word or point to a word that corresponds to a word given by a voice synthesizer. The Speak and Spell educational device is just a hint of breakthroughs in the voice field. The voice feature may be especially helpful in the teaching of English as a second language.

The computer can also be used for writing activities. For example, writing assignments are often disliked by students. Along with other factors, rewriting and reorganizing parts of the paper are points of student frustration. According to Ahl, "Writing and rewriting by hand is really difficult for a kid" (1, p. 89). Especially for middle school students, the ability to make corrections, move sentences around, delete or add letters, words, or paragraphs on the computer can make writing enjoyable.

Fourth graders in eleven suburban Los Angeles schools and middle school students in a New York school are using word processing microcomputers to write and rewrite sentences, paragraphs, and essays (12). In at least one Milwaukee area school, word processing on a microcomputer is used to prepare camera-ready copy for the school newspaper. In a Chicago area high school, the writing center has 15 microcomputers with word processing programs. This is the same as the number of micros in the math-science center. Elementary word processing programs are available for most computers at reasonable cost.

Many professional writers have indicated the ease and speed which the use of word processing has brought to their task. Pournelle, for example, commented, "This [computer] made it easier to write science fiction." (9, p. 19). All major newspapers use word processing computers for writing, editing, and laying out pages. Observations indicate that writing on a word processor is performed differently from writing with paper and pencil: "Let the ideas flow; refine, move, polish, and edit later." Will students be ready for this?

The computer is also capable of keeping records for teachers. Numerous available programs will compute the readability of a text based on any of the popular readability formulas. The reading level can be computed just by typing in the selected passages. In contrast to the tedious hand calculations, this process may make use of the formulas too easy. Smith and Kepner caution against inappropriate use of the formulas on mathematics texts and other special materials, for example (11). It is important and to remember that the formulas were developed for standard prose.

Another exhausting teacher task is the grading of student essays. After much work on developing algorithms for evaluating students' writing, Jaycox noted that shortcomings are due to "problems in developing software acceptable to teachers" (5, p. 38). The problems center on varying grading criteria used by different readers. Slotnick found it possible to write a grading program that imitated a particular teacher's grading process (10). The program examined the errors noted by the teacher on several writing samples, and it was then able to apply the criteria to predict grades given by the teacher on subsequent samples.

To summarize, computers provide language arts and reading drill for students on an individualized basis, and they belong in the language lab. Students should also be introduced to word processing, the current writing tool in many businesses and writing establishments. Finally, computers can make teacher grading and record-keeping less tedious.

References

1. Ahl, D. "Interview with Gordon Bell." *Creative Computing* 6, no. 4 (April 1980): 88–89.
2. Allee, J. G., Jr., and Williams, R. L. "A Challenge for the Language Arts CAI Developer." *Creative Computing* 6, no. 9 (September 1980): 120–25.

3. Bencivenga, Jim. "Electronic Editing as a Tool." *English Journal* (January 1982): 91–92.

4. Heuer, R. "Reading Comprehension for the SOL-20." *Creative Computing* 6, no. 4 (April 1980): 36–39.

5. Jaycox, K. M. *Computer Applications in the Teaching of English.* Urbana, Ill.: University of Illinois, Department of Secondary Education, 1979.

6. Mason, G. E., and Blanchard, J. S. *Computer Applications in Reading.* Newark, Del.: International Reading Association, 1979.

7. Poulsen, G., and Macken, E. *Evaluation Studies of CCC Elementary School Curriculums, 1975–1977.* Palo Alto, Calif.: Computer Curriculum Corp., 1978.

8. PLATO Elementary Reading Staff. *Elementary Reading on PLATO IV, 1977.* Urbana, Ill.: Computer-Based Education Research Laboratory, 1977.

9. Pournelle, J. "Writing with a Microcomputer." *On Computing* 1, no. 1 (Summer 1979): 12–19.

10. Slotnick, Henry B. "An Examination of the Computer Grading of Essays." Ph.D. dissertation, University of Illinois, 1971.

11. Smith, C. F., Jr., and Kepner, H. S., Jr. *Reading in the Mathematics Classroom.* Washington, D.C.: National Education Association, 1981.

12. Toch, Thomas, "Sophisticated Microcomputers Used to Teach Students to Write." *Education Week* 1, no. 19 (February 2, 1982): 13, 16.

13. Williams, R. L., et al. *English Usage Exercises.* 3R Software, P.O. Box 3115, Jamaica, NY 11431.

8. The Computer in the Social Studies

Daniel L. Klassen and Don G. Rawitsch

A COMFORTABLE FIT

Teachers are often fearful of accepting new educational technology because they believe that the innovation may not totally apply to the currently acceptable content and methods, and it must therefore be forced to "fit in." Such is not the case with the computer and social studies. Although at first glance the computer may seem to fall entirely within the domain of the mathematics teacher, a closer look at the objectives of social studies teachers shows that the computer fits into their classrooms just as easily.

First, social studies introduces the student to social events and trends. One of the most influential of these developments during the twentieth century has been the growth and resulting effects of technology. At the heart of the current technological revolution stands the computer, which has made so many other advances possible. The importance of the computer's role in this revolution of automation, communication, miniaturization, and computation is reason enough to introduce students to the origins and impact of this mind-expanding device. Coincidentally, the computer happens to be one of the easiest examples of modern technology to bring live into the classroom now that personal computers are conveniently sized and reasonably priced.

Second, the social studies teacher is interested in introducing students to the social scientist's method of inquiry, an intellectual tool that can be applied to many other endeavors. Not only does the computer allow the student to examine a larger quantity of information at one time than ever before possible, but its advanced speeds allow time for many more exploratory attempts to find patterns and relationships among a large collection of information items.

Third, a major goal of social studies is to provide the student with the information and skills needed to participate meaningfully in a society of democratic decisionmaking and power-sharing. One of the keys to the acquisition of power is control of information, and computers are well equipped to facilitate such control. An understanding of the abilities and limits of computer use will be as important to the citizens of tomorrow as is an understanding of the use of the vote and group influence to the citizens of today.

After starting in the laboratory, computers have since moved steadily into industry, government, education and, finally, the home. Their importance as a social phenomenon, a tool of inquiry, and a key to power makes them a ripe topic for many areas of the social studies curriculum.

CHANGES IN COMPUTER USE SINCE 1970

Computer use in the social studies at the precollege level has remained uniformly low since the first instructional application in the 1960's. For example, the first national survey of computer use in education conducted in 1970 found that only 3 percent of all instructional computing occurred in the social studies. A followup survey in 1975 showed that this particular use had increased by only 1 percent (1).

Similar evidence of low usage was found in the 1977 National Survey of Science, Mathematics, and Social Studies Education. Table 1 shows the frequency of use of various types of equipment and supplies in social studies classes in grades 10 to 12. Only 3 percent of the social studies teachers surveyed claimed to have used a computer or computer terminal, whereas 74 percent reported that computers and computer terminals were not needed (6). Data from other grade levels show a similar pattern (see Table 2).

Although computer use in social studies has remained disappointingly low, some hope for a future increase can be found in these data. The number of teachers reporting that access to a computer or computer terminals is needed but not available suggests that expanded availability, brought about by low-cost microcomputers and time-sharing systems, may produce more computer use in the social studies classroom.

In addition, the growing number of computer-based social studies applications and the development of easy-to-use authoring languages may help make the computer a more friendly and useful tool in the social studies.

TABLE 1
FREQUENCY OF USE OF VARIOUS TYPES OF EQUIPMENT AND SUPPLIES
GRADES 10–12 SOCIAL STUDIES CLASSES

Manipulative Materials	Not needed	Needed but not available	Use less than 10 days	Use between 10 and 50 days	Use more than 50 days	Missing
				Percent of Classes		
Learning kits	43	28	19	6	1	3
Games and puzzles	29	20	34	13	1	2
Maps, charts, globes	12	9	17	33	28	1
Copies of original documents	23	19	34	19	4	1
Computer or computer terminals	74	20	3	0	0	3
Reference books	3	8	23	39	27	1
Paperbacks	11	15	24	34	15	2
Artifacts, models	38	27	22	7	2	3
Photographs, posters	11	16	34	23	15	2

SAMPLE N = 490

SOURCE: National Science Foundation. *The Status of Pre-College Science, Mathematics, and Social Science Education: 1955–1975.* (Washington, D.C.: Government Printing Office, 1977.)

TABLE 2
FREQUENCY OF USE OF COMPUTERS AND COMPUTER TERMINALS
IN K-12 SOCIAL STUDIES CLASSES

Percent of Classes

Grade Level	Not needed	Needed but not available	Use less than 10 days	Use between 10 and 50 days	Use more than 50 days	Missing	
K–3	84	6	1	1	0	7	N = 254
4–6	74	15	2	0	0	8	N = 281
7–9	78	18	2	1	0	1	N = 453
10–12	74	20	3	0	0	3	N = 490

SOURCE: National Science Foundation. *The Status of Pre-College Science, Mathematics, and Social Science Education: 1955–1975.* (Washington, D.C.: Government Printing Office, 1977.)

APPLICATIONS OF COMPUTER USE
IN THE SOCIAL STUDIES

Introduction to the Computer as a Laboratory

Unlike many sciences, social studies has seldom provided students with a laboratory experience—an experience which allows them to conduct experiments, examine and analyze data, or construct and examine models. In part, the lack of a laboratory experience in social studies instruction is due to the very nature of the phenomena of interest—nations and economic systems cannot be brought into the laboratory, for example. But, this lack is also the result of the difficulty social studies students often have in dealing with quantitative data. In addition, most precollege social studies teachers lack a quantitative orientation to their subject area.

Fortunately, the computer can help overcome some of these barriers by providing an "environment" in which students can analyze data, construct and manipulate models, and test hypotheses. Through the use of simulation and data analysis, the computer becomes a laboratory to social studies students.

Simulation—Personal Role Playing

Role playing is a common strategy used in social studies teaching. Activities can be devised in which the student takes the role of a political candidate in a mock election, a witness to a crime in a staged fight, or a dictator in a controlled classroom. In all these cases, the main purpose is to have the student experience situations that others in a society may face in order to better understand the actions and feelings of others.

The computer is helpful not only in setting up experiences in which the student can play a role, but in providing experiences that otherwise could not be simulated in a school building. It provides a representation of reality based on a model of the relationships between an individual and the human and physical environment. The computer user takes the role of that individual, reacting to computer-presented situations by making decisions.

In the computer simulation OREGON, for example, the student takes the role of a pioneer traveling west in the 1840's (4). Using a limited amount of money, the student must manage a supply of food, clothing, ammunition, and the like, and react to such events as bad weather, wagon breakdowns, bandit attacks, and geographic obsta-

69

cles. Adding to the fun and realism of the simulation is a feature in which the student's skill with a gun for hunting and protection is determined by the speed and accuracy with which she or he can type simple shooting sound words (such as bang) at a moment's notice as requested by the computer. It is no simple task to complete the 2,000-mile journey alive, as the real pioneers found out a hundred years ago.

The POLICY simulation calls for students to take roles representing special interest groups in the national political arena, such as business, labor, or the military (4). Each group has a certain amount of influence to use to get particular policies passed. After each round of intergroup bargaining, the computer keeps track of how each group has distributed its influence and which policies have enough influence behind them to pass. Then the computer evaluates the state of the nation as a function of the policies passed, as measured by 18 socioeconomic indicators. Through this process, students learn not only the value of bargaining and compromise, but also the potential impacts on the society that can result from a combination of policies enacted simultaneously.

A number of role-playing simulations such as the two just described have been created for computer implementation. They are often based on models backed by extensive research into historical events, economic trends, and political records. When using such a computerized simulation, it is important to place more emphasis on the student's experience than on the computer's actions, which serve mainly to stimulate the student's creative and analytical powers.

Simulation—System Models and Games

Another exciting and promising use of the computer to enhance instruction in social studies classes involves the use of another type of instructional simulation and games. Elementary and secondary social studies teachers are familiar with this approach to instruction; in fact, nearly 90 percent of all social studies teachers (K–12) report using noncomputer simulations and games (including debates and role playing) on a regular basis (6).

Computer simulation provides operating models of a physical or social system; whereas games are competitive interactions among participants to achieve specified goals. Since they involve competition, games are often highly motivational for students—especially those in which the student competes against the computer. When combined, simulation and games provide a powerful learning tool. In the social studies, simulation and games allow students to explore and discover cause-and-effect relationships; to develop and try out strategies; to develop decisionmaking skills; and to learn the operation of social, economic, and political systems.

Computer-based simulation and games differ very little from noncomputer simulation and games. Computer simulation makes it possible, however, for students to examine more complex models and provides a very fast and convenient way to explore relationships within operating models. Computer games in the social studies often allow a single student to engage in a learning activity and provide an exciting new element of competition—beating the computer. This is especially true at the elementary school level.

Computer use in the elementary and secondary social studies classroom usually involves the use of a simulation or game. In recent years, a number of interesting instructional simulations and games have been developed for use in these classes. They include CIVIL, CRIMEX, ELECT1, ELECT2, ELECT3, ENERGY, GHETTO, LIMITS, and USPOP (4).

Data Analysis

One way in which the computer has proven itself an invaluable tool is in the storage and handling of data. With a computer, students can store data, selectively retrieve it, sort it, and analyze it in a fraction of the time required by manual methods.

In data analysis, the "real world" is represented by a set of data—a data base—describing some aspects of that world—voters, citizens, cities, nations, crimes—or some other units of analysis. These units of analysis or variables can be described in a number of different ways, thus allowing the student the opportunity to compare and contrast and look for relationships. Through data analysis a student conducts "experiments" with the data searching for relationships and testing hypotheses.

Despite its value in the area of data analysis, the computer has not been used to any real extent for this purpose at the precollege level. This approach is, however, very common at the college level. It is hoped that social studies teachers will come to realize the instructional benefits associated with this approach and will begin to use the computer to apply it in the classroom. With the development of quantitatively oriented instructional materials such as those developed by the Social Science Education Consortium (5) and the continued advancement of computer technology to provide an easier-to-use and more "friendly" environment for both students and teachers alike, this use of the computer can be expected to increase in the years to come.

OTHER COMPUTER USES IN THE SOCIAL STUDIES

Information Storage and Retrieval

Computer-based information storage and retrieval is really just a subset of data analysis. It is identified separately here because it represents an area of growing computer use in the social studies.

Computers are very effective and efficient machines for storing and searching through large volumes of data. This feature allows teachers and students to conduct selective searches upon demand. Although teachers and students regularly consult various sources for information, until recently they have had to find the needed information in catalogs, bibliographies, and printed records, which has often required tedious and time-consuming searching through files, libraries, and indexes. Now, teachers and students in social studies classes are beginning to enjoy the advantages of having information available in the computer.

One typical use of the computer in this subject area is to provide occupational and career planning information. Students in social studies courses are often encouraged to examine occupational opportunities and the computer has proved to be a valuable tool in this effort. A number of computer-based career planning and occupational information systems have been developed and are in use to assist students in learning about present and future educational or career opportunities and to make them aware of occupations they would find personally satisfying. Such systems store and retrieve vast amounts of information and sort quickly through the data to find those with certain characteristics prescribed by the student. All this is done within the context of an interactive dialogue between computer and student. Some systems even allow the student to explore a variety of educational and training opportunities and to ask for information about scholarships (3).

Social studies teachers use information storage and retrieval features to help them maintain instructional objectives, student records, and inventories of instructional materials. Using systems like ERIC to locate needed information, both students and teachers are beginning to gain access to a wide range of instructionally useful information systems.

Computer-based information storage and retrieval represents a significant instructional opportunity in the social studies, and as a result, its use is expected to increase in the future.

Drill and Practice

In the early days of instructional computing, computers were heralded as devices which would save the teacher the time and effort usually devoted to routine matters such as quizzing students on material presented in class. Fortunately (in the authors' opinion), a wider variety of activities has been developed for classroom use. However, drill and practice continues to be a viable application of the computer.

In the social studies area, factual topics such as geographic features and the succession of U.S. presidents have often been the subject of drill programs. The computer poses a question which the student attempts to answer. If the answer is incorrect, the computer often gives clues to help on the next attempt. If the answer is correct, the computer may follow with additional information related to the initial question.

With the advent of personal computers (table-top size), a wider variety of visual features is now available to enhance drill exercises. The addition of color, sound, and graphics to the computer terminal used by the student makes it possible to accompany the questions with pictures, maps, animated diagrams, and even music. These are far more interesting than the typical list of written questions previously used in drill-and-practice activities. New computer features also have the advantage of providing a more exciting reinforcement to the student when answering questions correctly, thereby helping to increase motivation.

The Computer as a Manifestation of Technology

When thinking about computer use in the classroom, the teacher is likely to take the approach in which the computer is used as a tool in learning activities but only described verbally when covering its applications in, and impact on, society. It is much more effective, however, to use the computer to illustrate the latter concepts as well. The computer in the classroom can act as a live example of what computers do in society, or it can generate impacts on students in the same manner as it can in real life.

One dramatic negative impact of the computer has been to open the door to an entirely new area of criminal activity, computer-related crime. A resource package entitled "Computer-Related

Crime" uses the program COMCRIM to demonstrate for the student how computer procedures and coding can be altered to produce an undesired result in the handling of financial accounts (4). The examples given are simplified enough so as not to be usable on any real business computer, but the program stresses the point that an understanding of computer misuse is essential to appreciate the importance of safeguards against such activity.

The program HARLIE carries on conversations with the student, using each student response as a key for producing an appropriate computerized response (4). A live demonstration of the potential for artificial intelligence, it has a far greater impact on the student than mere reading abut the topic.

In situations where several schools use the same computer system, probably via telephone lines, computerized message services are usually created to facilitate communication between the users. This is a good demonstration of the impact of computerized communications and a glimpse of what the future holds for the average citizen. Writing letters, and indeed much of the printed word, may become obsolete in an age when many people are interconnected through a computer network.

The computer has great potential as a tool for helping the student learn about a variety of subjects. In the social studies classroom, however, it should not be overlooked as an effective way to teach about the computer itself.

THE ROLE OF THE SOCIAL STUDIES TEACHER IN DEVELOPING COMPUTER LITERACY

An earlier article in this monograph describes the concept of "computer literacy." This concept transcends any single instructional application, such as computer programming or computerized simulations, and refers instead to an entire collection of computer-related understandings, skills, and attitudes that the student can acquire.

It would be traditional to assume that a teacher in an area such as mathematics would take the lead in instituting computer literacy in a school curriculum. Social studies teachers have just as important a role to play in this area, however. Indeed, two of the categories of cognitive objectives for computer literacy listed in the earlier article—Applications and Impact—fall more readily into the social studies area.

A most effective way to design a computer literacy curriculum would be to create a team teaching effort between mathematics and social studies teachers that would integrate the presentation of both the technical and social aspects of computing. The partnership shown between teachers from diverse disciplines, as well as the locating of computing equipment for demonstrations in both areas of the school building, would emphasize to students the connection between technological advancement and social impact. In schools where such a team arrangement is not possible, an effort could still be made to teach computing topics in mathematics and social studies classes in conjunction with each other so that students would experience them simultaneously.

At the same time, it is important to recognize that the understanding of the computer, like the understanding of our political or economic systems, is not just a topic of facts to be covered in a single unit during one year of the student's education. Computing activities in the social studies classroom should be introduced numerous times in the elementary and secondary curriculum. Nor do they need to be isolated as a "computer day." Computer use to simulate an election or to quiz on state capitals adds to the student's development of computer literacy just as lectures on computing careers do.

The major goal is to help students understand the relationship to each other of the many computing activities they undertake, and to help students feel as comfortable with the computer in their lives as they do with the automobile or the television. This can be accomplished in the social studies classroom as well as in any other part of the school.

References

1. Bukoski, William J., and Korotkin, Arthur L. *Computing Activities in Secondary Education.* Washington, D.C.: American Institute for Research, 1975.
2. Diem, Richard A. *Computers in the Social Studies Classroom.* Washington, D.C.: National Council for the Social Studies, 1981.
3. GIS (Guidance Information System), Time-Share Corporation, Hanover, NH 03744.
4. MECC System Library. *Social Studies.* St. Paul: Minnesota Educational Computing Consortium.
5. Project QUESST, Educational Resources Center, 855 Broadway, Boulder, Co 80302.
6. Weiss, Iris R. *Report of the 1977 National Survey of Science, Mathematics, and Social Studies Education.* Research Triangle Park, N.C.: Center for Educational Research and Evaluation, 1978.

9. The Computer in the Fine Arts

Henry S. Kepner, Jr.

Often the computer is considered a piece of technology that should be classified with the physical sciences and mathematics. Its capabilities to serve as a tool for creative human thought cannot be limited to this narrow field, however. Furthermore, the low cost and accessibility of microcomputers have made them tools of the fine arts in schools, not just in isolated institutes.

This article classifies some uses of the microcomputer in art and music. Despite the few details provided, the reader should know that much is being done in both fields in elementary and secondary schools throughout the country. The article also includes a brief mention of computer uses in the theater.

ART

Once again, with the advent of new materials and creative individuals who use them for expression, the definition of art is expanding. Computer graphics is the new medium of this expression. Examples are available daily through television. Cartoon shows—especially the Saturday morning series—and commercials include animation generated through computer graphics. Most big-league sports arenas have large display boards that are computer-controlled. These changeable message boards are becoming highly popular atop buildings and on billboards.

There are two distinct methods of generating a computer image for transfer to paper, TV monitor, or electronic sign. In the first method, referred to as the "digitized image," an "image is provided as data to the computer [which is] external to a computer program" (5, p. 45). In this method, someone plans out the representation on a grid which corresponds to the number of dots or lattice points on the video screen or sign. Thus, the form is first sketched on paper and then translated to computer data for reproduction on the monitor. The first inexpensive microcomputer to give students the opportunity to graph easily in color is the Apple II computer. Students can choose a 16-color low resolution display with a 40 x 40 matrix or an

8-color 280 horizontal x 193 vertical high-resolution display. The author has worked with third graders who have generated an untold number of images by plotting out their picture using the 40 x 40 or 280 x 193 array. These students have created words, lettering, maps, and such favorite friends as Snoopy and the Hulk.

The second method of generating a computer image uses algorithms or procedures which are part of a computer program. An early procedure studied by elementary school students is random art. Using the computer's random number generator, students program the computer to randomly select a point on the screen and an available color or character. These images are projected on the screen at a rapid rate. Since the background "color" on the screen is a color choice, the user notices that points disappear. A run of this program fascinates both children and adults.

The grid structure of the display unit forces computer graphics to be mathematical in nature. Thus, work with equations of known figures—lines, circles, sine curves—is helpful in gaining mastery of the potential of computer art. One form of art "is distinguished by the fact that it is precisely the equations themselves which give the figures beauty and appeal" (8, p. 105). Numerous examples of art based on equations of curves, polynomial functions, and periodic functions (sine, cosine) are widely displayed in the art world (14).

Students do not have to know mathematical equations to develop a curve, sketch, or cartoon character. Several companies have developed graphics tablets on which figures may be drawn with an electronic pen. This electronic board transfers the image to computer memory. The electronically stored information can then be represented on the video monitor or on paper.

Using the mathematics of movement in the plane of three-dimensional space, students have been extending the work with Escher-like art (5, p. 49). This movement allows designers to build a graphics model of an object and then rotate it to see it, in perspective, from any point of view. The procedure is common practice in architecture, aircraft, and auto design, and also in tool and die design. More recently, chemists have been using this design method in creating potential molecular structures such as DNA-type chains.

The field of graphics communication has also moved to computer-based artwork and production. A recent issue of *U & lc* (Upper and Lower Case), the international journal of typographics, was devoted to acquainting practitioners with the new technology and its functions (11). The opening editorial of a later issue set the focus: "New kinds of typesetters and electronic page makeup devices, graphic creation stations and display terminals, even the electronic/digital typesetting of color halftones, are commercial realities." (12, p. 3). Thus a major concern of the graphics communication profession is the adequate training of entering students in computer uses.

Computers and display units are now available at reasonable cost for the study and construction of visual representation. They allow the introduction of movement to previously static art forms. Students are already exploring these capabilities in the school setting. Since the art is generated by a computer program and associated data, the expense of the art form is relatively cheap. And the computer can be used over and over again—it is not a consumable supply.

MUSIC

To the surprise of many people, the computer is opening a whole new accessibility to music for adults, students, and the school curriculum. Existing computer programs allow the user to compose music for up to 16 voices, play music entered in the computer, display notes on a video screen, edit existing music, and hear music through stereo amplifiers (6).

Electronic music has been in existence for nearly half a century. Now, a special form has come into its own—computer music. According to Kitsz, "Computer music is fully electronic sound in which the actual waveforms, envelope (electronic equivalent of an embouchure), volume and so on have been calculated and created by a computer under the composer's direction." (4, p. 27).

For instructional uses, several companies and individuals have developed curriculum packages that provide computer-assisted drills. The drills are usually intended for individual student work following classroom instruction. Programs currently in use drill on these topics: stating interval distance, writing or identifying scales, recognizing rhythm patterns, recognizing whole- and half-steps, identifying which note shown on the screen was not played, identifying which note in an observed phrase was played wrongly, and stating the type of triad played. These drills permit individual response to the correspondence between sheet music and the music heard. They are a major extension of the group response to a record or to a teacher at the piano for individual students. They greatly enhance the opportunities for learning how to read sheet music and to recognize patterns, especially for nonperforming students. Most of these programs are available for the Apple II, as well as other computers.

Clark, et al. provide another drill example of computer-aided sightreading (2). They describe and list a program that generates 10 random notes on the staff following the student's choice of clef. The program, written for the TRS–80, Level II, 16K RAM memory, times the student's attempts to sightread using keys labelled DO, RE, etc.

For many students, the opportunity to compose music through the computer opens a new area of exploration. As a nonperformer, the author has thrilled at composing a short score and hearing it played, and after each playing has made modifications to improve the quality. On a small scale, this experience parallels that of most composers as they hear a composition performed for the first time. For example, on the television special honoring his eightieth birthday (aired in November 1980), Aaron Copland noted: "The ecstasy of hearing a piece you composed for the first time. You think you know what it was like, but you're never really sure!"

In music appreciation, the example of a theme is presented frequently, but it is often difficult for the untrained ear to pick up a repeated segment by listening to a full orchestral performance on record or tape. When segments of such a piece are stored in a computer, teachers have control over which parts, or voices, to play. They can play a segment repeatedly, each time adding or deleting other voices so that students can follow a major or minor thread in the score.

For the musician, the computer is a new instrument to be challenged—one that tirelessly plays what the composer writes, modifies, and embellishes. For the educator, the computer is an instructional tool that provides individual drill on music fundamentals and appreciation skills, even for the nonperformer. For the nonperformer, the computer presents an opportunity to be involved in music construction.

Certainly, the collection of educational activities in music is unfinished.

THEATER

For the theater, the major uses of the computer focus on management and script and stagecraft directions. The computer is an ideal tool for listing the inventory of company sets, costumes, props, lights, and the like. On the other hand, the computer as a word processor (see the discussion in the arictle "The Computer in Business Education and Careers") is ideal for making changes in scripts, stage directions, and lighting sequences. These changes can be made electronically without the need to retype the entire copy manually.

In recent professional performances, for example, computer-controlled lights were needed to provide the intended effect. Frequent, complex lighting changes could not have been made manually with the required precision. Although such electronics are not available for school theater performances at this time, the basic electronic units may be within budget limitations in the future.

References

1. Borry, L. "Meet the Music Teacher's New Assistant—A Microcomputer." *AEDS Monitor* (October–December 1979): 21.
2. Clark, D. B.; Wilkins, C. T.; and Tuma, D. T. "Computer-Aided Sightreading." *Creative Computing* 6, no. 6 (June 1980): 84–88.
3. Ettinger, L., and Rayala, M. "Computers in Art Education." *Computing Teacher* 8, no. 4 (1980–81): 24–29.
4. Kitsz, D. " A Short History of Computer Music." *Microcomputing* (December 1980): 27–30.
5. Kolomyjec, W. J. "The Appeal of Computer Graphics." In *Artist and Computer,* edited by R. Leavitt. Morristown, N.J.: Creative Computing Press, 1976.
6. Mercuri, R. T. "Music Editors for Small Computers." *Creative Computing* 7, no. 2 (February 1981): 18–24.
7. Micro Music, Inc. 213 Cambridge Dr., P.O. Box 386, Normal, IL 61761.
8. Schmucker, K. "The Mathematics of Computer Art." *Byte* 4, no. 7 (July 1979): 105–116.
9. Tubb, P. "Apple Music Synthesizer." *Creative Computing* 6, no. 6 (June 1980): 74–83.
10. ——. "Musical Subroutines." *Creative Computing* 8, no. 3 (March 1982): 124–32.
11. *U & lc* 7, no. 2 (June 1980).
12. —— 7, no. 4 (December 1980).
13. Waite, M. *Computer Graphics Primer.* Indianapolis: Howard W. Sams and Co., 1979.
14. Walter, R. "Creating Computer Art." *Creative Computing* 4, no. 3 (May–June 1978): 84–86.

10. The Computer in Business Education and Careers

Mel Hynek and Eric P. Schluter

One of the schools' responsibilities is to prepare students for future employment. A major objective of high school business education curricula is to provide students with a background enabling them to enter the business world upon graduation and to function effectively on the job. To accomplish this, business education students need to gain insights into the business world they will enter. Thus there is a need for interaction between the schools and employers concerning what should be taught in business education curricula.

The widespread use of electronic computing equipment has affected the duties of many white-collar jobs. Consequently, business-related occupations are becoming more dependent on electronic systems for information to enable them to perform their daily job functions. An indication of this conversion is the marketing thrust of the Tandy Corporation's Radio Shack computers. The TRS-80 microcomputers were originally built for the computer hobbyist, but as a result of recent model changes the major market is now businesses at all levels. This increased use of electronic equipment in business occupations will significantly influence the high school business education curriculum.

What will be the impact of the present-day electronic revolution and possible future technology on students' lives? No one has all the answers to this question, but this article discusses some directions employers have taken or are likely to take in the future that will have an impact on business education as we know it today.

THE CURRICULUM

Accounting Methods

The majority of accounting functions in medium to large businesses are automated. With the development of microcomputer technology, small businesses are rapidly changing from manual to automated accounting methods. Students enrolled in high school accounting courses therefore need to become familiar with computerized accounting procedures and processes. Textbooks and instructional accounting computer software packages are available today that are designed for high school level students. Some examples are *Computer Oriented Accounting* (13), *Automated Accounting for the Microcomputer* (2), *Microcomputer Oriented Accounting: A CAI Approach* (14), and *Micro Integrated Computerized Accounting Systems* (12). These accounting packages allow the student to analyze accounting transactions, code the transactions on input forms, and enter the data into the computer for processing. After processing, the student corrects any coding or keying errors as one would in a business situation. The computer packages are usually written in FORTRAN or BASIC programming language and are available at a reasonable cost. Schools with access to microcomputers or time-sharing computer systems should explore the possibility of incorporating computerized accounting concepts into the regular accounting courses. If some type of computer access is not available, computing equipment vendors are usually willing to bring equipment into the classroom and demonstrate accounting applications for students. Field trips also provide students some exposure to computer concepts and methodology without hands-on experience.

A trend in the teaching of accounting at the high school level is to stress student understanding of accounting concepts and the relationship of accounting to management decisionmaking. This approach deemphasizes the drudgery of extensive paper-and-pencil exercises and calculations. According to Rose, accounting, the language of business, should develop in students an understanding of how owners and managers use accounting information to make decisions (16). Accounting teachers need to help students by developing a process that will teach decisionmaking skills. The process should include analyzing the problem, generating alternative solutions, and choosing from alternative solutions.

Keyboarding

Keyboarding (which is not the same as typewriting) is a popular concept in business today. It is defined as the act of entering alphanumeric data on a desk-top unit. The data is often transmitted to a computer for storage or manipulation. Keyboarding has expanded into other career areas beyond the secretarial/clerical area. For example, through keyboarding accountants enter journal transactions into the general ledger, airlines handle requests and reservations, insurance agents make inquiries and changes in customer poli-

cies, bank loan officers find out information about customers' savings accounts. As Goodrich states:

> In considering the present applications of keyboarding, one cannot help but remember when typewriting was a skill required only by secretaries. While those days are not very far behind us, they are just that—behind us! Gone are the days when the typewriting course was designed primarily to prepare for secretarial jobs. Today's keyboarding course must prepare men and women for their careers, any one of which may have a typewriter-like keyboard in it. (8)

What should be the business education teacher's role in dealing with this new concept of keyboarding? The skills emphasized in traditional typewriting courses continue to be essential. They include learning keys by the touch system, developing speed and accuracy, proofreading, following directions, and meeting deadlines.

Goodrich describes additional skills needed for keyboarding:

> Careers requiring keyboarding need employees who will competently enter data not only from written material but also from orally supplied material. In both cases, the employee will frequently be required to mentally transform the information given into a form acceptable for entry on the keyboard. There is a need for a better understanding of composing functions, so more composing should take place in the first keyboarding course. (8)

Textbooks such as *Keyboarding for Information Processing* (9) are available. However, there is more to developing a keyboarding course than the selection of a textbook. Dickey-Olson suggests that students completing a keyboarding course should be able to perform the following skills:

- Demonstrate the correct "touch" system techniques for operating the alphanumeric keys.
- Demonstrate the correct "touch" technique to be used on a ten-key numeric pad.
- Demonstrate a straight-copy speed of 30 words-per-minute and an accuracy level of not more than two errors-per-minute.
- Demonstrate the ability to work from typed and rough-draft material.

- Demonstrate the ability to detect and correct errors in completed work (proofread).
- Demonstrate the ability to follow oral and written directions.
- Demonstrate the ability to backspace and correct errors.
- Transfer the "touch" system of keyboarding skills for most of the electronic automatic repetitive keyboards currently on the market. (6)

Business education teachers should tailor their keyboarding course objectives to their respective schools, taking into account such things as grade level and academic abilities of students, and equipment availability. It should be emphasized that the skills associated with keyboarding do not necessarily mean the acquisition of additional new equipment.

The Office of the Future

Any business education teacher who has found it difficult to accept technological changes in the past will find a look into the future to be almost beyond belief. A major target of the electronic revolution is "the office." Why? According to the Stanford Research Institute, during the ten-year period from 1960 to 1970 factory-worker productivity rose 83 percent while white-collar productivity increased 4 percent (20). Dartnell's 1981 cost estimate for a dictated business letter transcribed and then typed on a traditional keyboard is in excess of $6.60 (15, p.128). For the office of the future, the name of the game will be increased productivity.

There has been a great deal of predicting about the form the office of the future will take. The following pages discuss several areas on which there appears to be consensus.

Word Processing Systems

The major office revolution centers on the inclusion of word processors (also called text-editors). By early 1981, over one million word processing units were in use, with an additional 1.5 million anticipated by 1985. By 1983, the demand for word processing operators is expected to exceed 2.5 million individuals (10). The features of a word processor include text creation, text revision, file maintenance, file merger, and electronic mail. The text is entered and stored electronically through a keyboard; it is viewed on a video screen. Additions, corrections, deletions, and insertions can be made electronically. Only then is a copy printed on paper, shipped electronically, or stored permanently. With one typing of a form letter, an

"individualized" letter can be produced for each customer, agent, or creditor based on information on the individual stored in a large data base.

In the office of the future, word processing systems will be taking on a new look. According to Adler:

> It is clear that office automation, with its increased use of the mini and micro computers, is moving closer to data processing from a technological viewpoint (1).

Microcomputer systems are able to perform common data processing functions such as payroll, accounts receivable, accounts payable, and general ledger. They can also generate various reports for management while handling word processing responsibilities such as text editing, data entry, and information retrieval. The International Word Processing Association projects that in the 1980's, automated text-editing equipment (basically microcomputers) will be as common to offices as the electric typewriter is today. Kelly Services predicts that by the end of the century, "over 70 percent of the nation's work force will be in . . . the automated office" (10).

Electronic Mail

The office of the future will also utilize electronic mail, which Edwards defines as follows:

> Electronic mail refers to the delivery, via electronic means, of messages that would otherwise be transmitted physically through the postal system or verbally via the telephone. As such, electronic mail may be considered a faster, cheaper, or more convenient alternative to the postal system or voice network (7).

For the most part, electronic mail systems are still in the prototype stage. However, such systems and services are already available. They have gained some intensive use in Great Britain and in a few large U.S. corporations. A page of copy can be sent coast to coast via electronic mail at a cost of less than a first-class stamp. It is estimated that, by 1985, 23 percent of the current amount of U.S. first class mail will be distributed electronically (15).

Electronic Filing of Documents

Closely associated with electronic mail is the electronic "filing" of documents which can be retrieved, updated, or deleted electronically at a later time. Many insurance companies currently use this procedure—storing, updating, and reporting policies and claims on videoscreens, and generating paper copies only for legal records.

What impact can these changes have on the business education curriculum of the future? Present business education instruction centers around the use of paper, whereas the office of the future will tend to be paperless. Will teachers be preparing students for future jobs in which they will probably never type on paper, fold a letter, address an envelope, erase, make a carbon, or file a piece of paper?

The Human Factor

Ergonomics, human engineering, anthropometics. These words are mentioned with increasing regularity in the computer industry as operators, system planners, union management, government agencies, and equipment manufacturers struggle to assess the physiological and psychological impact of computers on the people who use them (17). The office of the future will undoubtedly utilize equipment designed to reduce eyestrain, neck, shoulder, and back ache, and fatigue. Design changes will include such features as higher CRT resolution printing, less screen reflection, tilting and rotating CRT screens, detachable low-profile keyboards, document-holding capability, and adjustable workplace furniture.

The Human Voice

The office of the future will use the human voice as an input vehicle to computerized systems. Miller predicts that

> In the future—perhaps as soon as the mid 1980's—speech recognition will replace touchtone telephone input as the preferred input capability to computer systems. (11)

Strategic, Inc., a San Jose, California, research and consulting firm, has predicted that sales of speech synthesis equipment in the information processing and consumer business will grow from $23 million in 1981 to $495 million in 1985 (19). This firm also predicts that high-quality speech will become available on chips costing less than $15 in large quantities.

Talking to the computer rather than keyboarding to the computer—what are the possible implications of this development for the business teacher. In the past it has been difficult, at best, to place students with limited secretarial skills such as typing in clerical positions. Voice recognition systems which are already available have allowed quadraplegics, disabled persons, and others with limited manual dexterity to work effectively with computer systems.

These systems will greatly expand the employability of students possessing few, if any, keyboarding skills.

Personal Qualifications

What kind of person will work in the office of the future? What duties will she/he have? There is not much consensus on these questions, but we do know that this person is likely to be someone who is different from the person now known as a "secretary."

According to Stewart:

> The day may not be too far off when secretarial jobs will require a master's degree in business administration and be regarded as an entry-level step into management . . . there will be more creative-type positions, fewer dog-work-type tasks, and there will be far more tasks. (18)

These people will be heavily involved with information management. Part or their duties will be to help others analyze available information and prepare reports.

Cunningham has yet another view:

> The secretarial station will become part of the corporate information bank or the data bank that is kept regarding all corporate activities. The secretarial station will become an information management terminal. (4)

Already many companies have prewritten programs and data storage that allow secretarial personnel to generate reports, summarize information, and produce business predictions. Companies are developing new secretarial-related job descriptions which include increased responsibilities and salaries, and new job titles. Many old job titles are being changed to the new "administrative assistant." Historically, business education has not attracted much of the male school population. Higher salaries and new job responsibilities may attract more males to this traditionally female area of the curriculum.

Productivity

Will the office of the future attain the desired increased office productivity? Yes and no. For the most part, the high-technology office equipment has lived up to claims made by the respective manufacturers. Why, then, have not all companies seen increased office productivity after installing it? Most failures can be attributed to "human" rather than "machine" problems. Companies that have not correctly addressed the issue of the relationship of people to evolving office technologies have failed to achieve increased office productivity. According to Anderson, it is important not to regard people as extensions of office machines. Assembly-line-type demands should not be placed on office workers. It is management's responsibility to give workers a variety of duties which allows them to use the skills they possess (3).

Business education teachers have the responsibility of informing their students of the likely changes in future office environments. Anderson explains one of the most crucial tasks business educators can perform to prepare students for the future. That is, when students leave the educational setting, they must do so with the knowledge that this is only the beginning of what is to come in office technology and the acceptance of lifetime changes that will be demanded of them (3).

At the same time that business educators are faced with the dilemma of how to prepare their students for the future, they must also prepare themselves for the changes in business education that most certainly will come.

CAREER AWARENESS

Before students begin training for a career, it is important for them to make an informed career choice. Despite wide use, most people still do not know how computers operate or what procedures are necessary to make them useful and productive tools. An important first step is an understanding of computer operation and the tasks to be performed.

Books, filmstrips, movies, and videotapes are now available on the high school level, which deal with computer design and operation, data processing applications, and computer-related careers. A variety of information concerning data processing careers and salaries is also available from such organizations as the local Better Business Bureau and the American Federation of Information Processing Societies. Publications such as *Datamation* supply up-to-date information on careers (5). Classified advertisements are an excellent source of information and can be used as a starting point for students researching the data processing job market. All these materials are valuable resources for enhancing career awareness. However, none of these resources gives students any direct knowledge of computers. This gap can be filled by enlisting the help of the business community. A well-planned field trip can provide students with a closeup look

88

at computer hardware and the interaction with personnel in a variety of careers, as well as the chance to observe some computer uses.

A field trip can offer tremendous educational opportunities if the proper groundwork has been laid. For example, business personnel must be informed of the students' backgrounds so that their explanations and remarks will be appropriate for the audience. It is also important that the organizer of the field trip convey its goals and the types of situations that students should be able to observe. And not only the teacher conducting the field trip should be prepared; the students should also be prepared if they are to receive the maximum benefit from the experience.

The teacher can provide much of the preparation by presenting the concepts of data processing, and exposing students to some of the terminology they are likely to encounter. More specific preparation can be provided by inviting someone from the proposed field trip site to the school to discuss from the proposed field trip site to the school to discuss the company and the role of data processing in its operations.

As important as the preparation is the followup. Student reports on the field trip give them the opportunity to organize the information they have received. A followup speaker from the company can reinforce many things students have seen and heard, and give them an opportunity to clear up any questions they may have.

For any field trip experience, the first step is to establish contact with the right person. In small businesses, the appropriate person to contact is usually the owner or president; in large businesses, it is the director of data processing. It must be emphasized, however, that it is the teacher's responsibility to take the leadership role in providing preparation for everyone to ensure a successful experience.

DATA PROCESSING CAREERS

With the introduction of the computer into the business world, a new set of tasks developed, most of them centered on the functioning of the computer. As the number of individuals in computer-related jobs grows, clerical and bookkeeping positions are being phased out. What computer positions are now open to students?

Large Businesses

In large organizations the data processing employees tend to become specialists with expertise in a limited number of tasks. These organizations also present the opportunity for advancements and promotions, possibly to management-level positions.

In such business settings, the person who works most directly with the computer is the computer operator. Several levels of this position may exist. Beginning operators usually work with peripheral equipment such as card readers, tape drives, and printers. Experienced operators are at the computer console, responsible for the running of jobs and the resolution of problems which may arise. A high school diploma is the minimum requirement for the entry-level position, but some training at a technical school is preferred.

Another person who works closely with the computer, but in a much different capacity, is the systems programmer. The person in this position is responsible for maintaining the computer's operating system, a collection of programs which control the computer's functions. Such a position requires a good background in both hardware and software; it is usually filled by a college graduate with some courses in computer science.

The two positions just described are related to the functioning of the computer. The greatest number of jobs, however, are those concerned with developing applications for the computer. One such position is that of systems analyst. The systems analyst is a problem-solver on a large scale. He or she must analyze a general problem situation and devise a master plan for developing a data processing system which will best solve the problem. The systems analyst is the leader of a computer team responsible for developing and implementing that solution. Such a position usually requires a college degree. The systems analyst also needs an understanding of both business and data processing concepts, as well as the ability to work with people who have a wide range of company backgrounds and responsibilities.

One of the people helping to implement a data processing system is the computer programmer. The programmer develops solutions for specific problems, always following the master plan. This task includes designing the solution, translating the design into a computer program, and then testing and debugging the program. Although a two-year degree often qualifies a person to be hired as a programmer, a four-year degree allows the person to begin at a higher level or to advance more rapidly.

Small Businesses

As minicomputers and microcomputers have become available, and their cost has dropped, increasing numbers of small businesses have begun to use such equipment. These businesses include anything from a one-person shop on up. They have neither the need nor the budget for large data processing staffs of highly specialized individuals. In most cases they need one or two employees who can perform all the tasks required to use a small computer system. Such persons may not necessarily be required to design systems and write programs; however, they may need a knowledge of programming in order to modify programs purchased from outside sources to meet the company's needs.

CAREER TRAINING

For all business students, practice on word processors and learning to enter data through keyboarding will be beneficial. Availability of word processing programs for microcomputers makes such experience feasible. And the additional use of microcomputers for grade reporting, class lists, and attendance makes them a financially sound investment.

For students interested in computer operations, employment may be immediate upon high school graduation, or after one year of technical school. The necessary training requires the availability on a regular basis of a variety of equipment which very few high schools possess. The schools can, however, provide a general background in computers and their operation. In some cases it may then be possible to place students in summer or after-school intern positions with local businesses to provide actual hands-on experience.

For students interested in computer programming, there is no substitute for actual programming of a computer. The low price of microcomputers makes it irresponsible to deny students an opportunity to gain computer access. Rental of time-sharing equipment or off-time use of local business computers provides an alternative form of access.

When learning to program the computer, students should see and be expected to use good programming practices such as internal and external documentation. (See the article "Computer Science: A Secondary School Course.") The techniques of structured design, for example, have come into common use in the business community. Although this structure is more evident in computer languages such as Pascal and COBOL, it is a valuable concept for all business-oriented programmers. Yourdon presents a clear description of the concept (21, chapter 2).

Computer Languages

The choice of computer language for business education can depend upon many things. Very often a language is used simply because it is available. But if options exist, the choice should be based upon the uses for which the languages were developed and the advantages and disadvantages to students. Four commonly mentioned languages are BASIC, Pascal, FORTRAN, and COBOL.

BASIC is a language commonly used in schools and on many of the new microcomputers. It is an interactive language providing the user with immediate feedback. It is also fairly easy to learn, allowing students to write and run simple programs on the first day.

Pascal is also an interactive language which is increasing in popularity, especially in the colleges and universities. Although not quite as easy as BASIC, it is ideal for teaching the concepts and techniques of structured programming.

FORTRAN is a language well suited for use in the fields of mathematics, science, and engineering. Recently a structured version of FORTRAN was released, which is consistent with the current trend in business.

COBOL is a language developed for business applications. Although it is somewhat difficult, it is a trememdously popular language, especially among large businesses—thus creating a very good job market for COBOL programmers. It can also be made to conform to the rules of structured programming.

Many small businesses use RPG, a specific use language designed for generating reports. Because of its limited applications, it is easy but it does not require the student to learn how to program the computer.

Whichever programming language is used, the objective should always be good program design and good programming. (RPG does not conform to these requirements.) The language is just a tool.

CONCLUSION

All functions of business from accounting to management to clerical operations are being computerized. Business education teachers must keep abreast of these changes in order to provide students with the best opportunity for success in the business world. And they also need to update their own skills through in-service courses, professional reading, and on-the-job experiences.

References

1. Adler, Ira M. "Software for the Office of the Future." *Interface* (Fall 1979): 25–26.
2. Allen, Warren W., and Klooster, Dale H. *Automated Accounting for the Microcomputer*. Cincinnati: South-Western Publishing Co., 1982.

3. Anderson, Marcia A. "Addressing the Human Factor." *Word Processing and Information Systems* (September 1981): 54.

4. Cunningham, Sheila. "Word Processing Service Bureaus." *Interface* (Fall 1979): 28–29.

5. *Datamation.* Technical Publishing Co., 1301 South Grove Ave., Barrington, IL, 60010.

6. Dickey-Olson, Patsy A. "Keyboarding." *Balance Sheet* (November 1981): 91–93.

7. Edwards, Morris. "A Catalyst for the Office of the Future", *Infosystems* (December 1978): 42–43.

8. Goodrich, Elizabeth A. "Keyboarding: An Increasing Fact in Today's Society." *Business Education Forum* (February 1979): 15–17.

9. Hanson, Robert N., and Rigby, D. Sue. *Keyboarding for Information Processing.* New York: Gregg Division/McGraw-Hill, 1981.

10. Kelly Services. "Today's Changing Office." *Journal of Business Education* (April 1981): 271.

11. Miller, Frederick W. "Talk It Over with Your Computer." *Infosystems* (August 1978): 62–65.

12. Minnesota Educational Computing Consortium. *Micro Integrated Computerized Accounting System.* St. Paul: Minnesota Educational Computing Consortium, 1980.

13. Pillsbury, Wilbur F. *Computer Oriented Accounting.* Cincinnati: South-Western Publishing Co., 1974.

14. Pillsbury, Wilbur F., and Ripperger, William. *Microcomputer Oriented Accounting: A CAI Approach.* Cincinnati: South-Western Publishing Co., 1982.

15. Rider, Michael E. "Word Processing and Office Systems." *Balance Sheet* (December–January 1981–1982): 127–29.

16. Rose, Ginger A. "Teaching Decision–Making Skills in Accounting." *Business Education World* (November–December 1981): 18.

17. Sanders, Matt. "Executives Consider the Human Side of Computer Systems." *Modern Office Procedures* (December 1981): 56–64.

18. Stewart, Jon. "Computer Shock: The Inhuman Office of the Future." *Saturday Review* (June 23, 1979): 14–17.

19. Strategic, Inc. In *Word Processing and Information Systems* (September 1981): 8.

20. Yacht, Carol. "The Office of the Future, Today." *Balance Sheet* (September–October 1981).

21. Yourdon, Edward. *Techniques of Program Structure and Design.* Englewood Cliffs, N.J.: Prentice-Hall, 1975.

11. The Computer in Science

Ron Tenison and Henry S. Kepner, Jr.

The evidence of the past decade has shown the computer to be heavily involved in the physics and chemistry classrooms and laboratories of the university but virtually held captive by the math department of the secondary school. The presence of inexpensive micro-computer systems with graphics capabilities has made the computer a popular, if not necessary, tool in the science curriculum. Computer articles now appear in national physics and chemistry journals for secondary school teachers, and computer-related talks are much more in evidence on the programs of national and local conferences. Still, an all-too-common experience is to be approached by a science colleague at a local, or even national, meeting with the question "What do you do with a computer that you can't do with a calculator?" The answer is "A lot!"

Basically, there are four ways to use computers in the middle and secondary school science classrooms: teaching about computers, teaching with computers, using computers as an assistant, and using computers as a tool. The following uses started at the university, but they are now well established in many secondary schools throughout the country.

TEACHING ABOUT COMPUTERS

The use of the computer in the laboratory originated with its ability as a supercalculator as well as its ability to take on the tedious job of monitoring equipment and recording masses of data quickly or over a long time interval. Because of this, the student needed to know how to operate the computer equipment as well as how to write the programs to analyze the data.

For nearly a decade at Catlin Gable School, it has been typical for ninth grade classes to learn programming in the fall term so that students can use the computer to analyze lab data over the next three and a half years. Although the growth of the calculator industry has switched some of the original need for the computer to the smaller hand-held devices, there still remain many tasks where the students prefer a computer to their hand calculator. Most commonly these tasks involve large quantities of data to be output. Student control of computer calculations, data storage and retrieval, and printout is a valuable time-saving asset in our science curriculum. Certainly, the kind of data generated by the PSSC Physics tickertape labs or the CHEMS equilibrium lab computation are examples of complex analysis projects that students are asked to do. Without calculating devices, teachers take steps to shortcut some of the work, such as doing fewer runs for a narrower range of examples, or reducing the number of possibilities tried in searching for constant relationships. Over the years, we have found that the presence of computational devices has allowed us to do "more interesting problems," explore a wide range of relationships, and increase the efficiency of our in-class work. Often students are able to complete calculations as well as the experiment in the lab period, so that an initial discussion of the results can take place immediately following the experiment. At the very least, data and computed results can be entered on classroom data tables and likely measuring errors spotted by students in time to repeat the experiment while the equipment is still assembled. Students can be given the lab calculation procedure as a homework/ programming assignment along with a sample set of test data before the lab. This allows them to come to class with a program already on the computer (or programmable calculator) that is debugged and ready to use.

Another area where the teacher can teach students about computing machines is that of digital electronics, taught either as part of the physics course or as part of a full-scale electronics course. It is possible to deal with interfacing the computer to laboratory equipment for data recording or for condition monitoring and control. Very little of this kind of activity has taken place at the secondary school level, but it is common at the postsecondary level. Recently, however, a growing number of secondary students have sought information on how to use a personal computer to control lights and thermostats, and even to monitor the environment of an animal during training or behavior experiments. The use of analog-digital converters brings this task within the capability of science projects for independent students. Community resource individuals—parents, hobbyists, engineers, and merchants—are sometimes willing and helpful in this area.

TEACHING WITH COMPUTERS

The growing availability of inexpensive computers and computer systems with graphics capability has initiated the potential for several students to do computing work simultaneously during a class period. Through aggressive budgeting and long-range planning, many schools are accumulating a number of microcomputers or purchasing a small four- or eight-user time-sharing system. Through cooperative teacher planning, several computing stations can be available for a crucial lab lesson. This often involves wheeling microcomputers from the mathematics laboratory to the science room. In a reciprocal move, all computing power may be available to a math class on a different day. This flexibility is enticing a number of science teachers to consider teaching with the computer.

USING COMPUTERS AS AN ASSISTANT

There are a number of ways to use the computer as a teaching assistant, but the most common is through simulation. Many science concepts are difficult for students to experience directly either because of the cost, the large amount of time involved, or the lack of sufficient equipment. These experiences can be at least partially provided through a program that allows the student to interact with the computer: changing experimental conditions and watching the results. For example, students are able to do more experimental work with optics in physics. The cost of optics benches and the time required to perform a series of experiments are prohibitive. A student working on a project through the Oregon Museum of Science and Industry wrote a program which allows the user to define the shape, separation, material, and so on, of a lens or systems of lenses and arrange them graphically on the screen. The program then allows the student to specify the direction of incoming light and draws the path followed by the light as it is refracted by each lens in turn. Since it is possible to change virtually any condition about the lenses or the medium they are in, the possibilities for student exploration are extensive.

The graphics capabilities of many microcomputers have initiated several local projects simulating wave motion experiments. Variations of the sine curve generate many basic wave principles such as frequency, amplitude and interference, and can be demonstrated clearly on the video screen.

The Catlin Gable chemistry teacher recently returned from a conference where a program for qualitative chemistry was described. She is in the process of modifying the program for our computer. This simulation program, which is available commercially but is expensive at this time, allows the student to try to work out the identity of an unknown compound by specifying tests, reactions, or observable properties. The computer simulates the tests and, based on certain data, tells the student the results. The student continues to request specific information until s/he solves the puzzle. The program will be used as a preliminary to the CBA Unknowns lab and as a followup for students who have not yet grasped the idea of using compounds.

The value of a simulation is not limited to individual or small group use. It is an excellent lecture aid with visual examples and data generation providing immediate reinforcement on key points or instant results based on student questions. This capability interjects the "What-would-happen-if . . .?" interaction in a presentation. The ability to connect school television monitors to computers allows the teacher to have all students see computer-generated graphs or results simultaneously. The linking of two or three monitors to the computer is a technique frequently used for class instruction in Milwaukee area schools.

Another way that computers are being used as teaching aids is through tutorials. Computer tutorials can present information, monitor testing, and update records of student progress. We currently have computerized tutorials in programming, in some basic math skills, in error analysis, and in some chemistry topics. There is quite a potential for using this type of material for students who have math skills weaknesses or who need more exercises in a certain area, or for students who have been absent. In the state of Oregon there is a growing number of individualized, or continuous progress, courses.

Many computer tutorials are already available for purchase, especially in chemistry, and the number is growing. Not all of them are pedagogically sound, and some do not make very creative use of the computer potential. Some, however, are quite good, and most are at least usable. The article "Computer Software in Education," which appears elsewhere in this monograph, addresses the difficulties of developing educational materials for computer use. It is sufficient to note that knowledge of good teaching skills, strong programming competency, and a sensitivity to learner responses are necessary. Seldom are these skills found in one person.

At this time, most science programs are locally written. Through sharing, professional improvement occurs. Some of the most refined materials exist as part of the Huntington II materials and others reported through CONDUIT, a clearinghouse centered at the University of Iowa. As the number of computers in the schools has increased, the educational media companies have entered the market with computer software.

USING COMPUTERS AS A TOOL

There are several examples of this type of computer use. With the development of competency programs and individual educational plans, teachers are being directed to keep more student records. Thus it is not uncommon to hear the complaint "When do I get the chance to teach?" A common use is for test or worksheet construction. Teachers can keep files of questions and answers and select from them for inclusion in a test or worksheet. Often there is a need to make up a new test for students who were absent, or an extra worksheet for students who need a little extra practice. The advantage of the computer over a paper file is that teachers can select the questions and get a typed copy in a matter of minutes. Even the new nonimpact printer terminal can create a spirit master. It can also be used for word processing-type applications such as preparation of text materials which require updating and improving each year. Many small systems now have word processing software available at very reasonable costs, but even the standard editor that comes with the machine can save teachers a great deal of work. Those who are fortunate enough to have access to a quality hard copy terminal will find that the heavy load of college recommendations every fall can be eased as well.

CONCLUSION

The computer has entered the science curriculum. It is a combination of laboratory equipment, instructional assistant, and generator of scientific data for student exploration. Through student and teacher programming control, it is the most versatile tool in the science department. Both students and teachers can benefit from its power and speed.

12. The Computer in Middle School Mathematics

Vincent F. O'Connor

In the late 1960's schools began to acquire computer terminals for use in high school computer science courses. In most cases these terminals were used for only one or two classes a day, and since the computer science teacher was usually also a mathematics teacher, it was quickly seen that these terminals could provide a valuable tool for mathematics classes.

The computer could be programmed to generate arithmetic problems of a specific type; thus students who needed drill and practice were able to get immediate feedback rather than working an entire set of problems before finding out they had been practicing errors. It was also found that students were somehow motivated to do practice on the computer whereas similar written work was met with great resistance.

The computer was a tireless drillmaster, with the patience of a loving mother, the quickness of a master typist, the memory of an elephant, and the noise of a 1953 junker needing a tuneup. Students accepted criticism from the computer without flinching and were not embarrassed to make an error in front of it. Teachers found ways to personalize the experience by using students' names within the programs and by keeping track of student work, so that the next visit to the terminal could pick up where the last one left off. Problems of noise and lack of available hardware were minimized in light of the potential resource that the computer represented.

A decade or so later the hardware advances have widened the options for schools, neighborhood stores are selling home computers at prices within the price range of many families, and companies are selling computer programs ranging from simple games to complete drill and practice programs, even including a management system for keeping track of student progress. These factors have increased the use of computer technology in middle school classrooms and have sparked interest in applications at the elementary school level.

This article describes current and potential uses of computer technology in middle school mathematics classes in a nontechnical manner and independent of any particular computer system. It is hoped that these descriptions and examples of classroom uses will help teachers who have not had the opportunity to use a computer see the educational benefits lying beneath the surface—a surface which may make it seem to be just a toy or little more than fun and games. It is also hoped that through these descriptions and examples, teachers who have had some experience in using computers in their classes can see ways to increase their value.

THE COMPUTER: AN EDUCATIONAL TOOL

There are two distinct uses of the computer—as an educational tool and as a topic of instruction. Use as an educational tool capitalizes on the computer's characteristics to provide educational experiences for students. As a topic of instruction, the concern is to involve students in learning about computers and programming. As one might expect, there is some overlap between the two uses. Students learn about computers when using them for drill and practice, and they can gain valuable mathematical skills and concepts while writing computer programs. The primary objectives are clearly different, however, and the reader should have no trouble detecting when these overlaps occur. The major part of this article deals with the use of the computer as an educational tool rather than as a topic of instruction.

When mathematics teachers examine a new textbook, filmstrip, tape, workbook, or other type of educational material, they consider many factors. Will it motivate the students? Will it add to the variety of options available or is it more of the same? Will it help meet individual student needs? Certain computer characteristics lend themselves well to each of these concerns.

Motivation

In an age of electronic gadgetry and increasing sophistication among middle school students, the computer holds at least an initial fascination for many of them. This built-in motivation factor can stimulate students to do some drill-and-practice work or investigate some important concept without even realizing that it is "schoolwork." This work may take the form of a gamelike setting. For example, a student using the program GUESS tries to find the computer's secret number based upon clues given by the computer. Figure 1 shows a sample of the interaction between computer and student.

100

```
ENTER YOUR FIRST GUESS.

?   10

10   IS TOO SMALL.   GUESS AGAIN.

?   60

60   IS TOO LARGE.   GUESS AGAIN.

?   42

YOU GOT IT. AND IT TOOK YOU
ONLY 3 GUESSES ! ! !

DO YOU WANT TO TRY ANOTHER GAME?
```

FIGURE 1

In the example, this|student was quite lucky, guessing the number on only three tries. As students play this kind of game, they quickly develop better strategies and apply such skills as mental arithmetic and logic. It should be noted that neither the student nor the teacher needs to know how to program a computer to use this type of game. Similar programs are available on most computer systems and can be accessed quite simply.

Some drill programs incorporate a challenge or competitive element which encourages students to sharpen their skills in order to become the class champ. One example, the program SPEED, puts each student against the clock in a race to complete a number of multiplication problems. Students establish records for quickness in working up to 100 problems correctly. They select the number of problems they wish and are timed as they work them. If all of a student's answers are correct, her or his time is compared with the record for the number of problems. The name of the student who has beaten the record is put in a prominent place—until someone faster comes along. To renew student interest and to stimulate continued maintenance of skills, old records are erased on a regular basis (for example, monthly).

101

Individualization

Unlike a textbook or other printed material, the computer is capable of branching from one point to another, based upon student response. This can help individualize students' class work in several ways. The example in Figure 2 shows a student interacting with the computer program FACTOR. This program gives drill and practice in finding the prime factorization of numbers. It provides for individualization in three ways. First, problems are created that fall into five levels of difficulty. The student enters the program at the middle level and proceeds upward or downward based upon performance. Thus the student receives problems at an appropriate level and is gently nudged on to harder problems. Second, the computer's reaction is geared to fit the student's response. For example, the student who responds "2X9" when asked for the factors of 18 will be told that 9 is not prime and will be given another chance at the problem. The student who responds "3X6" when asked for the factors of 36 will be told that 3X6 is 18 and will be given the correct answer. Third, each time this program is run the student will be presented with a unique practice set. Problems are generated randomly within the format specified. Each student's practice experience is different from that of others in the class, and if a student uses the program again, the second set will be different from the first.

Figure 3 shows the computer program MILLI which gives practice in estimating lengths in millimeters. It illustrates another way that the computer can individualize student work. Note that at one point the student took too long answer the question. The computer is programmed to allow about 30 seconds per question. When the student exceeded that limit, the computer changed the problem. The computer can be programmed to pace student work; it can also be programmed to cut a student off after a given time period or when achievement indicates that further work would not be beneficial.

Variety

The computer can motivate student work and help tailor that work to meet individual student needs, but is it any different from an electronic textbook, a programmed textbook, or a filmstrip series? Many things which can be done using the computer cannot be accomplished in the classroom in any other way. For example, Figure 4 shows interaction between student and computer using a program to develop student skills in estimating and approximating.

102

```
HI, I'M YOUR FRIENDLY FACTOR CHECKER.  ARE YOU READY FOR SOME PRACTICE
IN FINDING FACTORS?  I'LL GIVE YOU SOME NUMBERS AND YOU TELL ME THE
FACTORS.  THEN I WILL LET YOU KNOW IF YOU ARE CORRECT OR NOT.


FOR EXAMPLE:  IF I ASK YOU FOR THE FACTORS OF 12
YOU TYPE IN:   2X2X3
REMEMBER TO PUT AN X BETWEEN FACTORS.
IF THE NUMBER IS PRIME, TYPE 'PRIME.'


HERE WE GO.........


WHAT ARE THE FACTORS OF 78?    2X39
39 IS NOT PRIME. TRY AGAIN.


WHAT ARE THE FACTORS OF 78?    2X3X11
SORRY, YOUR FACTORS TOTAL 66.  THE ANSWER IS 2X3X13.


WHAT ARE THE FACTORS OF 21?    2X1
SORRY, YOUR FACTORS TOTAL 2.   THE ANSWER IS 3X7.


WHAT ARE THE FACTORS OF 6?    2X3
CORRECT.  HERE IS ANOTHER NUMBER TO FACTOR.


WHAT ARE THE FACTORS OF 77?    11X7
CORRECT.  HERE IS ANOTHER NUMBER TO FACTOR.


WHAT ARE THE FACTORS OF 130?   2X5X13
CORRECT.  HERE IS ANOTHER NUMBER TO FACTOR.


WHAT ARE THE FACTORS OF 135?   5X3X3X3
CORRECT.  HERE IS ANOTHER NUMBER TO FACTOR.


WHAT ARE THE FACTORS OF 185?   5X37
CORRECT.  HERE IS ANOTHER NUMBER TO FACTOR.

WHAT ARE THE FACTORS OF 157?   PRIME
CORRECT.  HERE IS ANOTHER NUMBER TO FACTOR.

WHAT ARE THE FACTORS OF 177?   PRIME
SORRY, NOT THIS TIME.  THE FACTORS ARE    3X59

WHAT ARE THE FACTORS OF 104?   2X3X17
SORRY, YOUR FACTORS TOTAL 102.  THE FACTORS ARE    2X2X2X13

YOU HAVE COMPLETED 10 PROBLEMS, GETTING  6 CORRECT
AND 4 WRONG.

YOU ARE WORKING ON LEVEL 3 IN THIS PROGRAM.
```

FIGURE 2

```
THIS IS A MILLIWORM

<MMMMMMMMMMMMMMM MM M MMMMMMMMMMMMMMMMMMMMMMMMM MM MMMMMMM*P

HOW LONG, IN MILLIMETERS, IS THE MILLIWORM FROM THE
TIP OF HER TAIL (<) TO THE END OF HER NOSE (P)?

ENTER THE LENGTH, IN MILLIMETERS?    100

SHE'S SHORTER THAN YOUR GUESS.

ENTER THE LENGTH, IN MILLIMETERS?     80

SHE'S LONGER THAN YOUR GUESS.

ENTER THE LENGTH, IN MILLIMETERS?     88

GOOD GUESS, YOU'RE WITHIN  5 MILLIMETERS.

IT TOOK YOU 3 GUESSES.


THIS IS A MILLIWORM

<MMMMMMMMMMMMMMMM MMMMMMMM*P

HOW LONG, IN MILLIMETERS, IS THE MILLIWORM FROM THE

TIP OF HER TAIL (<) TO THE END OF HER NOSE (P)?

ENTER THE LENGTH, IN MILLIMETERS?

YOU'RE TOO SLOW!  THE MILLIWORM GOT AWAY—NO FISHING TODAY.

ANOTHER TRY (Y OR N)?


THIS IS A MILLIWORM

<MMMMMMMMMMMMMMMM MMMMMMM*P

HOW LONG, IN MILLIMETERS, IS THE MILLIWORM FROM THE

TIP OF HER TAIL (<) TO THE END OF HER NOSE (P)?
```

FIGURE 3

```
WHAT IS YOUR NAME? VINCE
VINCE, I AM GOING TO CHALLENGE YOU TO AN ESTIMATING CONTEST.  HERE ARE
   THE RULES:
           --I WILL GIVE YOU 10 PROBLEMS.
           --YOU MUST ESTIMATE THE ANSWER TO EACH PROBLEM.
           --TIME IS A FACTOR (EACH SECOND WILL COST YOU A POINT).
           --ACCURACY IS A FACTOR (FOR EVERY.10% YOUR ESTIMATE IS
                   OFF FROM THE ACTUAL AMOUNT YOU WILL LOSE A POINT).

YOU CAN SET YOUR OWN GOALS, BUT I CHALLENGE YOU TO COMPLETE
THESE 10 PROBLEMS WITH LESS THAN 150 POINTS!!!

GOOD LUCK VINCE
..........ROUND  1 ...........
 100           DIVIDED BY      243
YOUR ESTIMATE? .4
ELAPSED TIME: 3  SECONDS
ACTUAL         YOUR           MARGIN OF
AMOUNT         ESTIMATE       ERROR
 .411523        .4               2 %


WOW!!! THAT'S A FANTASTIC ESTIMATE, VINCE.
PREVIOUS SCORE.......... 0
SCORE THIS ROUND........ 3
CURRENT SCORE........... 3
```
```
..........ROUND  5 ...........
 960              TIMES            225
YOUR ESTIMATE? 20000
ELAPSED TIME: 8  SECONDS
ACTUAL         YOUR           MARGIN OF
AMOUNT         ESTIMATE       ERROR
 216000         20000           980 %


YOUR GUESTIMATOR NEEDS WORK, VINCE!!!
PREVIOUS SCORE.......... 28
SCORE THIS ROUND........ 106
```
```
..........ROUND  7...........
ESTIMATE THE TOTAL OF THESE NUMBERS
 770        2145         105         990        26
YOUR ESTIMATE? 3300
FASTER, VINCE, DON'T CALCULATE!  ESTIMATE!!!
ELAPSED TIME: 19 SECONDS
ACTUAL         YOUR           MARGIN OF
AMOUNT         ESTIMATE       ERROR
 4036           3300            22 %

PREVIOUS SCORE.......... 142
SCORE THIS ROUND........ 21
CURRENT SCORE........... 163
```
```
VINCE, YOU HAVE BEEN A GOOD SPORT.  I HOPE THAT YOU WILL SHARPEN YOUR
ESTIMATING SKILLS AND TRY THIS CHALLENGE AGAIN. TRY TO SET THE
RECORD AMONG ALL THE STUDENTS IN YOUR CLASS.
YOUR SCORE OF  297  POINTS IS AN AVERAGE OF  29.7  POINTS PER PROBLEM.
CHECK YOUR PRINTOUT FOR WAYS TO CUT THAT DOWN.

SUMMARY
ESTIMATES WITHIN 10%.................... 5
ESTIMATES OFF BY 50% OR MORE.......... 2
TOTAL SCORE ......................... 297
DO YOU WANT TO TRY AGAIN? NO

BYE--HOPE TO SEE YOU AGAIN SOON, VINCE.
```

FIGURE 4

This program puts students in challenging situations where they are to estimate some quantity and are to be scored based upon the time used and the relative size of the difference between their estimate and the actual amount. Students who take too long to respond are told:

DON'T CALCULATE! ESTIMATE!!!

Wild guesses receive the comment that the student's "GUESTIMATOR NEEDS SOME WORK." The challenge is set to allow most students to achieve initial success but then to urge them on toward better skills by improving their scores.

The fact that students are interacting with the computer in a situation where time is an important factor makes this drill effective; a workbook exercise of the same type would most likely result in calculations rather than estimations.

Simulations

Computer simulations are further examples of how computers can add variety to classroom experiences. By using the computer's capability to generate random numbers, programmmers are able to model real-life situations and allow experimentation with these situations using a computer. These simulated experiences can be used to advantage in the classroom to develop problem-solving skills, by providing opportunities for students to apply their mathematical skills, and by providing semiconcrete experiences to help students understand mathematical concepts. Figure 5 shows several runs of the popular program DRAG. This program simulates a drag race between two cars, one of which is designed by the student. The design has four factors: horsepower, rear end ratio, tire width, and tire diameter. Manipulation of these factors can improve the car so that it will beat the computer's car in a quarter-mile race. Middle school students react very well to this kind of experiment and will work hard at fine-tuning their dragsters. They may also race against each other. Thus the computer can be used simultaneously by a group of students—as racing teams, competing for the class championship.

Figure 6 displays a printout of a coin toss experiment simulated on the computer. Of course students could carry out this kind of experiment by tossing a coin 1,000 times. Having the computer make the coin flips through simulation, however, enables the students to concentrate on the data, make tables and charts showing the results, and look at questions such as "What was the longest string of heads?"

```
WELCOME TO THE DRAG STRIP.
WOULD YOU LIKE INSTRUCTIONS? YES
YOU MAY RACE AGAINST ONE OF YOUR FRIENDS OR YOU MAY RACE
AGAINST MY DRAGSTER.  YOU WILL BE ASKED TO DESIGN YOUR
OWN MACHINE, SPECIFYING HORSEPOWER, REAR END RATIO (X:1),
TIRE WIDTH IN INCHES AND TIRE DIAMETER IN FEET.
DO YOU WANT TO RACE AGAINST ME? YES
I WILL HAVE CAR #1
DESIGN CAR #2
HORSEPOWER = ? 675
REAR END RATIO = ? 5
TIRE WIDTH = ? 22
TIRE DIAMETER.= ? 3

GO


ELAPSED          CAR #1              CAR #2
TIME        SPEED   DISTANCE    SPEED   DISTANCE
(SEC)       (MPH)   (FEET)      (MPH)   (FEET)

  1.000     22.071    16.382    21.402    15.879
  2.000     43.575    64.783    42.354    62.869
  3.000     64.002   143.982    62.443   139.997
  4.000     82.939   252.079    81.321   245.728
  5.000    100.107   386.668    99.731   378.085
  6.000    115.356   545.024   114.508   534.782
CAR# 2 STOPS BURNING RUBBER
CAR# 1 STOPS BURNING RUBBER
  7.000    128.639   724.299   128.491   713.351
  8.000    139.186   921.158   138.247   909.629
  9.000    146.922  1131.340   143.962  1117.020
  9.860    151.810  1320.000   146.836  1300.670
             ### WINNER ###
```

```
DO YOU WANT TO TRY AGAIN? YES
DO YOU WANT TO RACE AGAINST ME? YES
I WILL HAVE CAR #1
DESIGN CAR #2
HORSEPOWER = ? 675
REAR END RATIO = ? 4.3
TIRE WIDTH = ? 24
TIRE DIAMETER = ? 3.2

GO


ELAPSED          CAR #1              CAR #2
TIME        SPEED   DISTANCE    SPEED   DISTANCE
(SEC)       (MPH)   (FEET)      (MPH)   (FEET)

  1.000     22.071    16.382    21.780    16.162
  2.000     43.575    64.783    43.059    63.957
  3.000     64.002   143.982    63.381   142.305
  4.000     82.939   252.079    82.370   249.510
  5.000    100.107   386.668    99.755   383.405
  6.000    115.356   545.024   115.376   541.503
CAR# 2 STOPS BURNING RUBBER
CAR# 1 STOPS BURNING RUBBER
  7.000    128.639   724.299   129.103   721.154
  8.000    139.186   921.158   139.963   918.923
  9.000    146.922  1131.340   147.994  1130.470
  9.858    151.762  1319.380   153.049  1320.000
                              ### WINNER ###
```

FIGURE 5

```
DO YOU WANT TO TRY AGAIN? YES
DO YOU WANT TO RACE AGAINST ME? YES
I WILL HAVE CAR #1
DESIGN CAR #2
HORSEPOWER = ? 675
REAR END RATIO = ? 4.3
TIRE WIDTH = ? 22
TIRE DIAMETER = ? 3

GO


ELAPSED        CAR #1              CAR #2
TIME      SPEED   DISTANCE    SPEED   DISTANCE
(SEC)     (MPH)    (FEET)     (MPH)    (FEET)

 1.000   22.071    16.382    21.402    15.879
 2.000   43.575    64.783    42.354    62.869
 3.000   64.002   143.982    62.443   139.997
 4.000   82.939   252.079    81.321   245.728
 5.000  100.107   386.668    98.731   378.085
 6.000  115.356   545.024   114.508   534.782
CAR# 1 STOPS BURNING RUBBER
 7.000  128.639   724.299   128.584   713.361
CAR# 2 STOPS BURNING RUBBER
 8.000  138.186   921.158   140.325   911.076
 9.000  146.922  1131.340   148.652  1123.430
 9.860  151.810  1320.000   153.674  1314.390
          ### WINNER ###
```

FIGURE 5
(Continued)

```
RUN COIN
HOW MANY FLIPS? 500
THHHHTHTTTTTHHTHHTTHHTTHTHTHHTHTHTHHTHHHTHTHTHTHTHHHTHHHHTTHTTTTTTHHHTTTHTHHT
TTHTHHTHHTHTTHTTHTHTTHHTTTTTHHHHHTHTHHHTHTTTHHHHTTTHHTHTTTHTHTTTHTHHHHTHHH
HTTTTHHHTTTHHTHHTHHHHHHTTTTTHTTTTHTHHHHHHHTHHHTHTTHHTHHTTTHHHHHTTHTHTHHTHHTT
HHTHHTHHHTHTTHHTTTTHHHTTTTHTTTTHHHHTHHHHTHHHTHHHTHTTTTTHHTHHTTHTHHHHHTTHTHT
TTTTTTTTTTTTHTTTTHHHHTTTTTHTTTHHTHTHHTHHHHTHHHTHTTTTTTHHTHTHHHHHHTTTHHTT
TTHTHTHTHTTTTTHHTHHHHTTHTHHHHHTTTHTHTHTHTHTHHTHTTHTTHTTTTTTTHTTTHHTHTHHHTHTTT
TTHTTHTTTTTHTHTTTTTHTTHHHHHHTTTTTHHHHHHHHHTHHTHHTTTHHHTHTHTHTTTTTTHHHTHT

HEADS...... 241 ....... 48.2 %
TAILS...... 259 ....... 51.8 %

READY
```

FIGURE 6

In both the DRAG and COIN programs students receive data from the computer. They then take the printout and examine it in a problem-solving setting. This type of use permits more student contacts with the computer than is possible with drill and practice by individual students.

CLASSROOM MANAGEMENT

Despite cost reductions in recent years, it is unlikely that all classrooms will be equipped with one computer for each student. More realistically, part-time use of a single computer will probably be the most that a middle school teacher can expect during the 1980's. When the terminal or miscrocomputer comes to the classroom, teachers will need to establish a student flow to the computer corner just as they do with a math-lab corner, a reading corner, or a cassette carrel. The difference here is that middle school curiosity will almost certainly result in a crowd of students trying to get their fingers on the keys. Students also need an orientation in the use of the computer. Programs that lend themselves to group participation can meet these two needs.

Nearly all students are familiar with the battleship game (Figure 7). A game with positive value in a mathematics class, it can be played with varying levels of sophistication and strategy from middle school to senior high school mathematics. Teachers can use a game like this, with rules that are simple and familiar to students, to give a large group orientation to computer use. After the large group introduction, student teams can go to the computer corner to play battleship. If each team has 5 players and plays the game 10 times, it is easy to identify a class champion as the team with the fewest guesses in finding the 10 battleships. After the initial novelty has subsided, it is not difficult to establish individual student use of the computer corner as a normal part of the class activity.

Figure 8 shows one possible extension of this introduction, the program DEPTH. This three-dimensional search game is very popular among students who have mastered the battleship game. Its popularity and success with middle school students illustrate how students can acquire rather complicated concepts at an intuitive level and then generalize them to other situations. Semiconcrete experiences provided by the computer terminal seem to enhance this process.

```
HI THERE    WHAT'S YOUR NAME? VINCE
DO YOU WANT ME TO EXPLAIN HOW YOU PLAY BATTLESHIP, VINCE? NO
DO YOU WANT A GRAPH TO WORK ON, VINCE? YES
 10          .   .   .   .   .   .   .   .   .   .   .

  9          .   .   .   .   .   .   .   .   .   .   .

  8          .   .   .   .   .   .   .   .   .   .   .

  7          .   .   .   .   .   .   .   .   .   .   .

  6          .   .   .   .   .   .   .   .   .   .   .

  5          .   .   .   .   .   .   .   .   .   .   .

  4          .   .   .   .   .   .   .   .   .   .   .

  3          .   .   .   .   .   .   .   .   .   .   .

  2          .   .   .   .   .   .   .   .   .   .   .

  1          .   .   .   .   .   .   .   .   .   .   .

  0          .   .   .   .   .   .   .   .   .   .   .

             0   1   2   3   4   5   6   7   8   9   10


THE BATTLESHIP IS IN PLACE.   TRY TO FIND IT.
? 5,5
A BOMB AT ( 5 , 5 ) MISSED THE SHIP BY  6.403 MILES.
TRY AGAIN
? 9,0
GOOD GRIEF...YOU HIT IT AND IT TOOK YOU ONLY  2  GUESSES.
DO YOU WANT TO TRY ANOTHER GAME? YES



THE BATTLESHIP IS IN PLACE.   TRY TO FIND IT.
? 5.5
A BOMB AT ( 5 , 5 ) MISSED THE SHIP BY  5.831 MILES.
TRY AGAIN
? 9,0
A BOMB AT ( 9 , 0 ) MISSED THE SHIP BY  1.000 MILES.
TRY AGAIN
? 8,0
GOOD GRIEF...YOU HIT IT AND IT TOOK YOU ONLY  3  GUESSES.
DO YOU WANT TO TRY ANOTHER GAME? YES



THE BATTLESHIP IS IN PLACE.   TRY TO FIND IT.
? 5,5
A BOMB AT ( 5 , 5 ) MISSED THE SHIP BY  3.000 MILES.
TRY AGAIN
? 5,8
A BOMB AT ( 5 , 8 ) MISSED THE SHIP BY  6.000 MILES.
TRY AGAIN

? 5,2
GOOD GRIEF...YOU HIT IT AND IT TOOK YOU ONLY  3  GUESSES.
DO YOU WANT TO TRY ANOTHER GAME? NO
```

FIGURE 7

```
RUN DEPTH

DEPTH CHARGE GAME

YOU ARE CAPTAIN OF THE DESTROYER USS VINCENT ADAMS.
AN ENEMY SUB HAS BEEN CAUSING YOU TROUBLE; YOUR
MISSION IS TO DESTROY IT USING DEPTH CHARGES.
SPECIFY THE DEPTH CHARGE EXPLOSION POINT WITH A TRIO
OF NUMBERS.   THE FIRST TWO ARE THE SURFACE COORDINATES
(FIRST E-W, THEN N-S).   THE THIRD IS THE DEPTH.

DIMENSION OF SEARCH AREA   (IF YOU'RE NOT SURE, TRY 10)?   10

YOU HAVE  4  SHOTS

GOOD LUCK


TRIAL# 1 ? 5,5,0
SONAR REPORTS SHOT WAS NORTHEAST AND TOO HIGH.


TRIAL# 2 ? 3,3,5
SONAR REPORTS SHOT WAS NORTHEAST AND DEPTH OK.


TRIAL# 3 ? 2,2,6
SONAR REPORTS SHOT WAS TOO LOW.


TRIAL# 4 ? 2,2,5

B O O M!!    YOU FOUND IT IN 4 TRIES!


ANOTHER GAME (Y OR N)? N
OK.  HOPE YOU ENJOYED YOURSELF.

READY
```

FIGURE 8

TEACHER RESOURCE

Thus far, each example of computer use has involved interaction between students and the computer. Another valuable computer use for instructional purposes does not involve direct student contact. It is to generate exercises and practice sets for teachers to give to students as place work or homework. This use can be especially valuable when it frees teachers for more work with individual students or for instructional planning rather than the tedious work of making up a sheet of problems. Figure 9 shows an example of teacher interaction with the computer that results in a word search puzzle based on a mathematics vocabulary.

111

```
### WORD SEARCH PUZZLE MAKER ###
THIS PROGRAM PREPARES WORD SEARCH PUZZLES FOR YOU.
YOU SHOULD HAVE A LIST OF WORDS TO TYPE IN.

YOU CAN SPECIFY THE LENGTH AND WIDTH YOU DESIRE,
AS WELL AS THE NUMBER OF WORDS.  YOU ARE ALLOWED
UP TO A 30 BY 30 PUZZLE WITH UP TO 50 WORDS.

AFTER THE PUZZLE YOU CAN OBTAIN EITHER JUST
A LIST OF THE WORDS USED OR THE WORDS
WITH THEIR LOCATIONS WITHIN THE PUZZLE.

INPUT WIDTH AND LENGTH? 15,20
NUMBER OF WORDS? 15
WORD# 1 ? MULTIPLICATION
WORD# 2 ? DIVISION
WORD# 3 ? SUBTRACTION
WORD# 4 ? ADDITION
WORD# 5 ? GEOMETRY
WORD# 6 ? ARITHMETIC
WORD# 7 ? MEASUREMENT
WORD# 8 ? PERIMETER
WORD# 9 ? CENTIMETER
WORD# 10 ? TRIANGLE
WORD# 11 ? EQUATION
WORD# 12 ? GRAPH
WORD# 13 ? COORDINATE
WORD# 14 ? COMPUTER
WORD# 15 ? CALCULATOR

ADVANCE THE PAPER TO THE NEXT PERFORATION
AND HIT THE RETURN KEY.
```

```
I V B C I T E M H T I R A V I R W F P Q
N K R L P W R G N Q H Y E O R A W B S S
C O O R D I N A T E N O I T I D D A A Q
P U K F R E L G N A I R T A X L K b B U
B R K R L S G F V G Y L D V R Q Y W S L
B E J T G P J X D I V I S I O N C O M V
T T M U L T I P L I C A T I O N B B G W
A U G G J Z N J M T N E M E R U S A E M
O P Z X T F S D N O I T C A R T B U S P
D M S Z K K X W B N O I T A U Q E M L H
S O T X V T A R E T E M I T N E C O B O
Q C V I P T A K Z M Y J P G R A P H L D
X B H F P R E T E M I R E P U G K F O M
X B R O T A L U C L A C C A H S O L E B
O W G V B G E O M E T R Y L U W C N M A
```

FIGURE 9

STUDENT PROGRAMMING

Students attending middle school in the early 1980's will probably encounter a highly computerized society when they leave high school. Recognizing this situation, the National Council of Supervisors of Mathematics has included the following comment on computer literary in a statement on basic skills:

> It is important for all citizens to understand what computers can and cannot do. Students should be aware of the many uses of computers in society, such as their use in teaching/learning, financial transactions, and information storage and retrieval. The "mystique" surrounding computers is disturbing and can put persons with no understanding of computers at a disadvantage. The increasing use of computers by government, industry, and business demands an awareness of computer uses and limitations.(1)

At the middle school level, the uses described in this article—drill and practice in mathematic using computers as a communications medium—can provide elements of such computer awareness with little additional explicit instruction. These beginnings can help students make informed choices about further work in high school and can reduce the possibility of their dismissing the study of computing because of fear or misinformation.

For some students, however, the interest in computers is so strong and the aptitude so high that many schools find ways to take them beyond awareness-level experiences into the initial stages of computer programming. These ways can take the form of a computer club, a minicourse in programming which is part of an exploratory program in the school, or supplementary work within the mathematics class.

Increasingly, many textbooks that teach programming in the computer language BASIC are providing teachers a rich resource for use with students and, perhaps more importantly, a means of developing their own background in computer programming. In some cases, students rapidly progress in programming beyond the teacher's expertise. Although this may present an initial risk to the teacher, it can be an enriching experience. It offers the teacher a rare opportunity to help develop student independence in the learning process. Rather than being the dispenser of knowledge, the teacher can participate in the learning process, learning and guiding the process in partnership with students.

One way to start students in programming is to give them a computer program to enter and run. Figure 10 is an example of a worksheet of addition problems along with a computer program to check the work. Students receive the worksheet to complete and then are told that they can check their work on the computer by typing in the program and running it. Specific directions for such a worksheet depend upon the type of equipment available and the amount of instruction students need or have already had.

Addition Worksheet   Name _____

Find the sums. Then check your work using the computer program on the right.

1.	4502 3998	2.	3076 2519
3.	6482 7583	4.	5671 3987
5.	9743 6475	6.	4325 3489
7.	2508 3799	8.	6428 9476
9.	1472 9615	10.	375 9654

```
Type:   NEW

Type:   ADDING

Type:   10 INPUT A

        20 INPUT B

        30 PRINT A + B

        40 GOTO 10

        50 END

Type:   RUN
```

FIGURE 10

Following this kind of beginning, students can proceed to modify existing programs or develop their own, focusing on a specific mathematics problem or concept. For example, the program in Figure 11 will produce multiples of 3. Given that program, students can be asked to change it to produce multiples of 7.

114

```
10 LET M = 3

20 LET T = 0

30 PRINT T

40 LET T = T + M

50 GOTO 30

60 END
```

FIGURE 11

CONCLUSION

Since the purpose of this article is not to go into the specifics of programming, but rather to illustrate the various uses of the computer in the classroom, an appropriate conclusion is a reminder that the distinction between using the computer as an instructional tool and the computer as a topic of instruction is not entirely clearcut. Just as students can learn certain things about computers when using them as a medium of instruction, so too can they deepen their understandings of mathematics and engage in some real problem-solving experiences when learning to do even simple computer programming. The teacher who has not yet explored this phase of computer use is urged to take advantage of whatever local resources are available to learn about programming and to seek ways to integrate this topic into the regular mathematics study at least as an enrichment.

Reference

1. National Council of Supervisors of Mathematics. "NCSM's Position Paper on Basic Skills." *Arithmetic Teacher* 25, no. 1 (October 1977): 19–22.

13. The Computer in Senior High School Mathematics

Henry S. Kepner, Jr.

The use of computing equipment in secondary mathematics is fast becoming a recognized strength. According to a major recommendation of the the National Advisory Committee on Mathematical Education:

> ... beginning no later than the end of eighth grade, a calculator should be available for each mathematics student during each mathematics class. Each student should be permitted to use the calculator during all his or her mathematical work ... (7)

Reinforcing this recommendation, data obtained in the Second National Assessment of Mathematics indicated that over 75 percent of 9-year-olds, 80 percent of 13-year-olds and 85 percent of 17-year-olds had access to at least one calculator. One-fourth of the 17-year-olds reported access to a computer terminal in school for learning mathematics (8, pp. 73-77). With the introduction of microcomputers, this computer access is growing dramatically.

Computers are effective tools in the learning of mathematics. They can aid concept development; they provide experience with iterative calculations; they are valuable in mathematical problem solving; and they are an effective tool in the generalization of mathematical results. This article addresses examples of such uses. Nor should the reader ignore the computer as an effective drillmaster and as a computational tool for many students. Earlier articles in this book cover these topics.

CONCEPT DEVELOPMENT

Student work on the computer can enhance mathematical concepts throughout the secondary curriculum. The *variable* used in algebraic notation can be developed by use of computer storage locations. Statements like READ X, PRINT Y, and IF $(A=O)$ THEN STOP are constructive examples of a machine location that holds a numerical value. The value can be entered or changed at any time. Using these programming steps helps students grasp the elusive variable concept.

The computer language assignment statement requires a word of caution to mathematics teachers. The statement LET X = A + B instructs a computer to retrieve the values stored in locations A and B, to add these values, and to store the sum in location X. The statement is not an equation. The quantities stored in A and B are preserved, but any prior value stored in X is lost. The statement LET X = X + Y is confusing to most students. It cannot be interpreted as an equation. It commands the computer to retrieve current values stored in X and Y and compute that sum. This sum is now stored in location X, destroying the previous value.

In dealing with absolute value, students have difficulties when variable quantities are involved. Most students can compute the absolute value of 3, -7, 0, or $-\frac{1}{2}$. Dealing with x, x+7, -3x-2 present challenging problems. Writing a program to evaluate -3x-2 for given values of x is advantageous for many students. Key statements like IF $(-3X-2)<0$ THEN —— and IF $(-3X-2)>=0$ THEN —— are valuable learning steps.

The concept of slope can be developed and reinforced through graphics activities on microcomputers, especially with a video display. Number theory concepts such as factors, multiples, and primes are ideal computer-enhanced topics.

Through widespread growth of computer use in business and statistical applications, the use of subscripted variables in matrices is crucial to many students leaving high school. A list of the N players on the basketball team can be stored under variable names P\$(1), P\$(2), P\$(3), ..., P\$(N). (A common computer notation, \$, indicates storage of character strings—letters and symbols—as opposed to numerical information. Location P will hold number data, P\$ will hold letters.) The shots attempted by each player can be stored in locations P (1,1), P (2,1), P (3,1), ..., P (N,1), respectively. Field goals scored can be stored in P (1,2), P (2,2), P (3,2), ..., P (N,2), and fouls stored in P (1,3), P (2,3), P (3,3), ..., P (N,3), respectively. This information can be indicated in Table 1. Student use of actual information makes this an appropriate, motivational assignment.

TABLE 1
SUBSCRIPTED VARIABLES

PLAYER	SHOTS ATTEMPTED	FIELD GOALS	FOULS
P\$(1)	P (1,1)	P (1,2)	P (1,3)
P\$(2)	P (2,1)	P (2,2)	P (2,3)
P\$(3)	P (3,1)	P (3,2)	P (3,3)
P\$(N)	P (N,1)	P (N,2)	P (N,3)

A sequence of statements like

```
FOR I = 1 TO N
PRINT P$ (I), P(I,1), P (I,2), P (I,3)
NEXT I
```

generates actual data in the form presented in Table 1.

The introduction of easy-to-use graphics capabilities on micro-computers presents a major opportunity for reinforcing concept development through graphic representation. Numerous game-format activities, such as Battleship or Target, provide excellent student experiences in graphing before introducing the formal Cartesian notation. The representations of both two- and three-dimensional settings are learning tools. Green Globs are the newest graphics instructional idea (1).

Learning about the trigonometric functions is now greatly enhanced with existing programs that plot a trig function, change the amplitude or period, and vary the domain or range of the graph. In particular, "Function Graphs and Transformations," a computer program, gives the user easy command over almost any manipulation conceivable (3). Each change can be shown separately or several can be placed on the video screen simultaneously for purposes of student generalization. Student graphing should not be eliminated, but after a few basic points have been checked individually, students should spend time observing the results of the computer-generated information. Their time is thus focused on observing, thinking, and finding patterns in contrast to the paper-and-pencil drudgery associated with graphing.

ITERATIVE CALCULATIONS

All fields of mathematics have important segments focused on iterative, or repetitive, processes. Although extremely important to mathematics and its applications, iterative processes have traditionally been ignored in the school curriculum. Because of a tedious procedure or lengthy computations, a formula is often substituted for an iterative concept.

The instructional example of compound interest is a case in point. The concept of compounding, paying interest on the amount accumulated at the start of each period, was difficult to show through paper-and-pencil calculations. Typically, two compoundings produced frustration. Now, the simple iterative program illustrated in Table 2 makes the concept clear by showing the principal at the end of each period. Table 3 illustrates sample differences between simple and compound interest. Excellent discovery and student discussion activities have originated from such data as that in Table 3. To this author, the work illustrated here provides much more conceptual information than the formula

$$A = P \left(1 + \frac{R}{M}\right)^{MN},$$

where P is the original amount invested.

TABLE 2
AN ITERATIVE PROGRAM—COMPOUND INTEREST

```
10   REMARK   COMPOUND INTEREST

20   REMARK   I = RATE OF INTEREST, A = AMOUNT INVESTED
         (PRINCIPAL

30   REMARK   M = COMPOUNDING PERIODS PER YEAR, N =
         NUMBER OF YEARS

40   READ I, M, N

50   READ A

60   FOR K = 1 TO M*N

70   A = A + A*(I/M)

80   PRINT K, A

90   NEXT K

100  END
```

TABLE 3
SIMPLE AND COMPOUND INTEREST FOR $1,000 AT 6.75%

	1 Year	10 Years	20 Years
Simple Interest	$1067.50	$1675.00	$2350.00
Compounded Annually	1067.50	1921.67	3692.82
Compounded Quarterly	1069.23	1953.00	3814.22
Compounded Daily	1069.82	1963.91	3856.94
Compounded Continuously	1069.83	1964.03	3857.43

Much work with polynomial functions occurs after excessive calculations, such as evaluating P(x) for many values of x. The computer routinely performs these evaluations over the prescribed values of x. Student and teacher time is then used to observe the values, generate conjectures, and apply the function to specific settings. Using the graphics characteristics, the user has the choice of examining numerical values in the $(x, P(x))$ form or viewing a graph of the function.

From this work, the precalculus concepts of partial sums, limits, and continuity are open to student exploration. Fossum and Gatterdam provide excellent examples of the instructional value of computers in the calculus arena (2).

Many of these concepts are no longer reserved for the advanced math student. At the junior high level, students should be able to approximate the area of a circle in a variety of ways. This is necessary to help eliminate the mystery of the formula πr^2. A relationship between geometric and arithmetic processes should be used. After a student has placed a grid of small squares on a unit circle and estimated the number of squares needed to cover the circle, the computer is ready as a refinement tool.

The refinement allows students to approximate the area by calculating the sum of the areas of the inscribed rectangles cited in Figure 1. The only tricky discussion for nonalgebra students is the calculation of the height of each rectangle, $\sqrt{1-x^2}$. With this work done, students will get better approximations by using 100, 1000, or more inscribed rectangles. The program in Table 4 responds to that request.

The data generated by this technique introduces basic concepts of convergence from geometric and arithmetic views simultaneously. Note to the reader: Using the approach illustrated, develop a conjecture for the area of an ellipse. Recall, an ellipse in standard position has the equation

$$\frac{x^2}{a^2} + \frac{y^2}{b^2} = 1$$

for the ellipse shown in Figure 2.

As indicated in the previous article on middle school mathematics, the basic concepts of probability and statistics can be developed intuitively by using a program to conduct a basic experiment repeatedly and record the frequency of results. This constructive approach to probability and statistics may be the way to provide *all* students with these needed basics of our society.

120

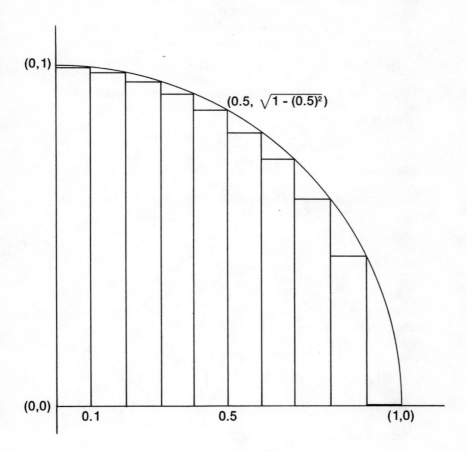

FIGURE 1
ESTIMATING THE AREA OF A QUARTER CIRCLE (10 INTERVALS)

TABLE 4
Area Of A Circle

```
10   PRINT "AREA OF A CIRCLE—EXPLORATION"

20   PRINT "HOW MANY RECTANGLES IN FIRST QUADRANT"

30   INPUT N

35   PRINT "WHAT IS RADIUS OF CIRCLE?"

40   INPUT R

50   REM A IS ACCUMULATED AREA OF INSCRIBED RECTANGLES IN
         QUARTER CIRCLE

60   A = 0

70   FOR I = 1 TO N

80   REM X IS X-COORDINATE OF UPPER RIGHT CORNER OF I-TH
         RECTANGLE

90   X = I*(R/N)

100  A = A + (R/N)*SQR(R↑2-X↑2)

110  NEXT I

120  PRINT "AREA OF CIRCLE IS APPROXIMATELY"; 4*A

130  END
```

122

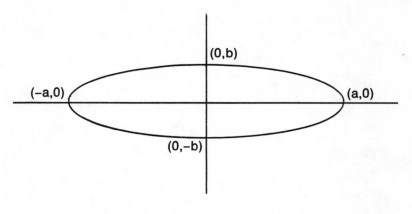

FIGURE 2

AN ELLIPSE WITH EQUATION $\dfrac{x^2}{a^2} + \dfrac{y^2}{b^2} = 1.$

PROBLEM SOLVING

Problem solving promises to be the major concern of mathematics education. The use of calculators and computers as mathematical tools will certainly reduce the time spent on computational drill. It is hoped that the time saved will be spent on student explorations of mathematical problems and applications.

Often students will find the computer a valuable tool in their problem solving. When a process has been established, student programmers can assign the computer to carry out a process for numerous cases or sets of data. Examination of the results will help evaluate the process.

Consider a simplified linear programming problem. A radio manufacturer learns from a marketing survey that she can sell 800 radios at $60 each. For each $2 price reduction, she can sell 50 more radios. What price yields the greatest gross sales? With the elementary computer program listed in Table 5, the student receives a listing of the gross sales for each price. The computer gives the student a valuable set of information. Now the student must read the table of data to solve the problem.

TABLE 5
A Simplified Linear Programming Problem

```
LISTNH
  10  REMARK MARKETING RADIOS
  20  REMARK P = RADIO PRICE, V= SALES VOLUME, G= GROSS
       SALES
  30  PRINT "PRICE   SALES  VOLUME      GROSS  SALES ($)"
  40  FOR K=0 TO 30
  50  V= 800 + 50*K
  60  P=60 - 2*K
  70  G= V*P
  80  P,V,G
  90  NEXT K
 100  END
```

RUNNH

Price	Sales Volume	Gross Sales ($)
60	800	48000
58	850	49300
56	900	50400
54	950	51300
52	1000	52000
50	1050	52500
48	1100	52800
46	1150	52900
44	1200	52800
42	1250	52500
40	1300	52000
38	1350	51300
36	1400	50400
34	1450	49300
32	1500	48000
30	1550	46500
28	1600	44800
26	1650	42900
24	1700	40800
22	1750	38500
20	1800	36000
18	1850	33300
16	1900	30400
14	1950	27300
12	2000	24000
10	2050	20500
8	2100	16800
6	2150	12900
4	2200	8800
2	2250	4500
0	2300	0

READY

Notice that the computer was not programmed to "solve" the problem. It provided data to the student. The student has the opportunity to use that information. Teachers often overemphasize the need to make the computer program carry through on the solving. The author suggests that this may challenge a student's programming techniques, but it is not part of the process of solving a particular problem. This extra step falls into the category of generalization.

With simple graphics commands on many microcomputers, the student can explore many functional relationships easily. The plotting of a curve tells much about a function, and its zeros, maximums, and minimums.

An example of nonnumeric problems is the mechanical mouse problem in which the student must develop a computer program to direct a mechanical mouse through a maze (5). The author has seen excellent student problem-solving performance in attacking this activity.

Another developing use of computers in problem solving is in the field of student-computer dialogues. These dialogues are written to help students derive proofs partly on their own. Through interactive questioning, the student develops a proof. The computer serves to react to the student's choices.

GENERALIZATION

A followup to problem solving is the mathematical task of generalization. Often, a procedure or algorithm works in some cases but fails to work in others. The computer provides an opportunity for testing generalizations. While not providing a guarantee, the ability to check a procedure for thousands of cases, instead of two or three, improves student confidence in the procedure.

When the procedure fails in certain cases, the exceptions can be analyzed. A classic example is the use of the quadratic formula. When students establish a computer program to solve any quadratic equation given the coefficients a, b, and c, they frequently do not include checks for $a = 0$ or negative discriminants. When generating solutions for many quadratics, the computer process will continually fail in these cases. To account for these, students must rethink the process.

CONCLUSION

The computer is a powerful tool in mathematics instruction. It should not be limited to a computer science course such as the one described in the next article. Students should develop minimal skills in using the computer to do mathematical work and check conjectures.

In the Milwaukee area, numerous secondary schools have two to ten microcomputers in their mathematics wings. The trend is accelerating nationwide. The question is, can we use this technology constructively?

References

1. Dugdale, Sharon. "Green Globs: A Microcomputer Application for Graphing of Equations." *Mathematics Teacher* 75, no. 3 (March 1982): 208–14.

2. Fossum, Timothy V., and Gatterdam, Ronald W. *Calculus and the Computer: An Approach to Problem Solving.* Glenview, Ill.: Scott, Foresman and Co., 1980.

3. "Function Graphs and Transformations." A computer program from Powersoft, Inc., P.O. Box 157, Pitman, NJ 08071.

4. *Journal of Computers in Mathematics and Science Teaching*, P.O. Box 4455, Austin, TX 78765.

5. Maniotes, John, and Quasney, James S. "The Mechanical Mouse." *Creative Computing* (May/June 1978): 46.

6. *Mathematics Teacher*, Special Issue on Microcomputers, 74, no. 8 (November 1981).

7. National Advisory Committee on Mathematical Education (NACOME), Conference Board of the Mathematical Sciences. *Overview and Analysis of School Mathematics, Grades K–12.* Reston, Va.: National Council of Teachers of Mathematics, 1975.

8. National Assessment of Educational Progress. *The Second Assessment of Mathematics, 1977–78, Released Exercise Set.* Denver: Education Commission of the States, 1979.

14. Computer Science: A Secondary School Course

Joseph W. Kmoch and Henry S. Kepner, Jr.

When a school first obtains access to a computer for classroom use, the most common inclination is to establish a course for students to learn about the computer's many facets. As a teacher assumes the responsibility for designing and teaching this course, numerous questions arise—What should be included in such a course? What kinds of teaching strategies can be employed? What kind of student reaction can be expected? These and related questions are discussed in this article.

GOALS AND TOPICS

There are three major goals for this course: (1) student problem solving with emphasis on the computer as a tool; (2) student mastery of elementary programming techniques helpful in using the computer as a tool; (3) student awareness of the role of computers in society—including major applications, societal impacts and issues, and career opportunities. The study of a high-level language such as BASIC, which at first appears to be the major goal of the course, is in fact a means to motivate problem solving and to investigate applications.

Several topics should be included in any computer science course; for example, the intensive study of a high-level language, a short unit on some low-level machine-oriented language, and an examination of the components of a computer and their interrelationships (see Figure 1). A focus on the solution of various problems provides a natural motivation for most of the computer language development within the course. Other topics to include are discussions of computer applications, careers in data processing, and the history of computing. If a course addresses only the study of a high-level language, then it becomes only a study of that computer language rather than an all-encompassing look at computers as tools in our lives today.

127

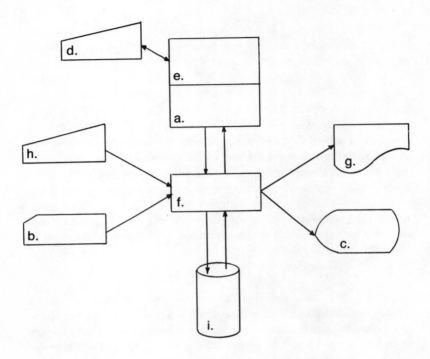

FIGURE 1
COMPUTER SYSTEM ORGANIZATION

a. Arithmetic-Logic Unit

b. Card Reader

c. CRT (Cathode Ray Tube)

d. Console

e. Control Unit

f. Primary Storage

g. Printer

h. Terminals (Keyboard)

i. Secondary Storage

SKILLS

A Beginning Language

For a given computer language, student problems must be carefully sequenced to allow growth in programming techniques. Therefore the study of the language should include simple calculations and simple input-output instructions (READ, PRINT, and INPUT); looping (GOTO, FOR-NEXT loops); conditional branching (IF-type statements); formatted output (PRINT-USING, FORMAT), subscripted variables (tables); and built-in functions (for example, character code, string functions, square root, and trigonometric functions). Variable types should include both numeric and string (for example, letters, words, and symbols) variables.

In using a particular computer language, the student should master programming techniques for carrying out the following tasks during the first semester: counting and totaling, multiple branching, and handling a list of data (such as creating a list, identifying an item in a list, and printing a list). These tasks require a knowledge of computer language syntax.

Problem Solving

The problem settings used throughout the course are an important consideration. Traditionally, teachers of these courses were mathematics teachers. Therefore, most of the problems tended to be math-oriented. In the real world, however, mathematical and science-oriented problem solving is but a small portion of computer use. Thus, teachers of this course should make an effort to expand the problem set to include nonmathematical as well as mathematical applications. Nonmathematical applications tend to be more meaningful to most students. Businesses deal with many situations that can provide opportunities for good, challenging problems—for example, payroll, inventory control, recordkeeping of store receipts, salesperson records, and maximizing profits. Consumer applications provide similar problems. Excellent advanced programming applications are available in assignments related to educational uses, computer games, simulation activities, art and graphics design, and music generation.

The most commonly programmed application in the business world is payroll, an area that has a special relevance to students because many have probably held or now hold jobs. This area is

129

often not fully exploited in computer science classes. A first problem could include straight-time hourly calculations with a second problem including overtime calculations. Such problems are good for starters but other aspects of payroll common to businesses can easily be included and understood by students. Some of these, for example, are calculating various forms of taxes (a particularly interesting one includes calculating federal withholding taxes by the formulas provided by the U.S. government); printing checks, including the amount of the check in words; calculating wages based on piecework or other incentives. Thus, payroll is a rich source of problems which are relevant, understandable, and often challenging to students of programming.

Another concern of many businesses is inventory control. A series of problems for this area could be developed, ranging from simply printing a report of inventoried products and their inventory values, to a more sophisticated program allowing interactive inventory changes as orders are processed and possibly even printing orders for products whose numbers fall below a certain minimum. The article "The Computer in Business Education and Careers" provides further development of business topics.

Consumer-oriented applications provide yet another large group of possible problem situations. Among these are family budgeting, calculating returns from savings and other investments, calculating monthly mortgage and other loan payments (including credit cards), situations involving fixed plus variable charges. An area that is particularly relevant to students involves high school credits, grade levels, grade point averages, and grade reports. Situations like these can be used to generate meaningful and challenging problems for students to savor.

Organizing sports statistics is one example of a problem that relates to student experiences and also lends itself to a data processing solution. The task of printing out player and team totals and averages in basketball or baseball is an excellent exercise in data processing. Work with student attendance and the standard business functions of the school provide additional problems for student exploration.

Mathematics concepts and applications form a rich source of problems useful in developing computer techniques. The articles "The Computer in Middle School Mathematics" and "The Computer in High School Mathematics" address these topics in this book.

Student assignments should often include several levels—the "minimum-required" level and perhaps several options, additions, and/or enhancements to the minimum problem. These additions can be parallel programs or simply additions to the original. Such a variety of problems allows the student to select assignments based on individual background and problem-solving ability.

Underlying all the aspects of a computer language study is an emphasis on problem solving. It is important that students understand that the study of computers is not an end in itself, but rather a vehicle used to check the problem-solving skills of the user. George Polya has outlined four essential steps to solve any problem: (1) understand the problem, (2) determine the procedure necessary to solve the problem, (3) perform the procedure, and (4) check the results (12). Writing the computer program itself involves only the third step in this process.

In the computer science course, the teacher usually starts by stating the problem and the procedure to be used. The student performs the procedure and verifies the results. As the course progresses, the teacher should seek to turn over more of the problem-solving activity to the student. This can be done by presenting less information and encouraging student independence. It would be unfortunate if the student's experience of an entire course consisted of watching the teacher organize and flowchart the problem and being assigned only to translate the flowcharted procedure into a functioning computer program. Every student should have the opportunity to completely solve a computer-related problem which is a challenge for that student.

Program Documentation

The process of program documentation is an important skill for students to develop. It helps the individual organize problem-solving thoughts and develop program writing style. Its use should be stressed from the beginning of the course. Students should experience three levels of documentation: (1) a verbal description of the problem, (2) a flowchart or similar diagram with an accompanying descriptive list of variables, and (3) remark statements within the program.

The verbal description should be a clear statement of the problem as viewed by the student—a statement understandable to someone without a computer background. As a reinforcement of the need for communication skills, this description should be a paragraph written in good, clear English with correct grammar and spelling.

The flowchart (or other structured format) is necessary to show the steps needed in the correct sequence to solve the problem. An accompanying list of variables describes the initial data and the intermediate results needed to solve the problem. Remark statements on the program listing are used to describe, in written form, the function of a single programming statement or a series of them.

Most programs written by students early in the course are very short (5 to 25 lines) and do not lend themselves to an extremely "structured" format. As students proceed further in the course (certainly in a second semester), they need instruction in program structure and style. As their programming expertise becomes more sophisticated, students should be presented with problem-solving situations of increasing complexity. Such problems should be constructed so as to make clear the need to write programs in clearly delineated sections (often called procedures). For larger programs, such a structure can be implemented by writing several of these sections as subroutines which are then invoked in a "main" procedure. An optimal situation is to present a problem with several options in such a way that the program completely solves the problem at a certain stage but then can be enhanced by writing the next option as a new subroutine which is then invoked in the main program.

An example of this type of problem is a simple payroll procedure. First, a computer program is written to do a simple hours-times-rate calculation and print the results. Then, a procedure can be added to calculate overtime (or commissions). Next, a procedure to calculate various taxes can be added. Enhancing the federal tax to include a graduated withholding tax (like that in IRS publication 16) can be next. Other procedures can include printing results in the form of a check, printing department totals, doing enhanced error checking (limits on gross pay output, numeric employee numbers). This program grows by adding new subroutines with the new features, rather than rewriting the whole program anew. Similar assignments can and should be built around other problem settings. Such multilayered problems give students a better concept of attacking large problems, help them organize solutions to problems, and provide an insight into the kind of job done by a systems analyst in the computer data processing field.

ADDITIONAL TOPICS

Three other topics should be included in a computer science course: computer system organization, applications of computers, and careers in data processing. Several times during the course, the teacher should use a diagram similar to Figure 1 for a nontechnical

132

discussion of the workings of the computer system used in class and in particular to focus on the interaction of the components as they are used. For example, such a diagram can be used to help explain system commands and the functions they perform—LOAD moves a program (file) from secondary storage (disk or tape) to primary storage (main memory) of the computer. Several of these discussions during the course will help students understand their use of various system commands and also when to use what command. Additionally, these discussions will help students understand how any computer processes information (that is, they will suggest answers to questions such as How do computers do what they do?).

Throughout the course it is also important to set aside time to discuss a variety of computer applications and careers in computer data processing. A varied set of problems including the data processing side of business, mathematics, science, consumer problems, and a study of surveys suitable for analysis by social scientists can provide many stimulating discussions of both applications and careers.

It is important to note that there is, and will continue to be, a much greater demand for individuals in data processing than in the scientific uses of computers. Examination of Sunday newspaper employment advertisements can initiate lively classroom discussion. Encourage students to further investigate career opportunities. Figure 2 shows one approach to such an investigation.

Career Notebook Directions

Make a career notebook that includes the following:

1. Twenty newspaper advertisements for jobs in the computer data processing field.
   a. Staple, glue, or tape each advertisement on notebook paper.
   b. Classify each advertisement as high-level training or low-level training.
2. Select one advertisement, call the company, and explore for the following:
   a. Job description, including:
      Responsibilities
      Complexities
      Working conditions
      Company benefits
   b. Educational requirements
   c. Special skills needed
   d. Salary range
3. Is this job personally compatible with your goals and ability? Why?

   Write sections 2 and 3 of this notebook in ink in grammatically correct form. Please use only one side of the paper.

FIGURE 2
COMPUTER CAREER REPORT

A variety of other topics can be undertaken beyond the first semester of such a course, or for more capable students during the first semester. Some of these topics are table (multidimensioned arrays) handling techniques, sorting lists, advanced search techniques in lists and arrays, use of subroutines to better organize (structure) programs, use of special functions such as random number generators in simulations, and character string manipulations.

STUDENT INTERACTION
AND INDEPENDENT LEARNING

One of the most rewarding aspects of teaching a computer science course is observing how students interact with their peers on an intellectual level. This interaction begins informally as students help each other solve small, simple problems and continues as they work with each other to constructively solve problems. Unlike many adults, students are eager to share their knowledge with anyone who will listen. Teachers can encourage and subtly guide this interaction so that students begin to work out most of their own problems. In addition to developing some important communication skills, this will allow the teacher to spend more time with students who are having a great many problems. The process can be more formally encouraged through the development of group projects. There are several reasons for making group projects an important portion of the course—for example, students need to learn how to deal with each other effectively and constructively, and the projects can increase student access to limited computer stations.

An inevitable result of this interaction and peer education is that some students will soon know more than the teacher does about at least some aspects of the computer and the programming language. It is important that the teacher not discourage students who reach this level. In fact, it is a good idea to foster such situations, as the following recent example illustrates. A student wanted to calculate and print a series of Fibonacci numbers whose size, at least apparently, exceeded the capabilities of the machine. The teacher knew of several possible techniques to extend the precision of calculations, but never had the time to explore these methods. After discussing some of these possible techniques with the teacher, the student went away with the charge to do some exploring and read some computer manuals. Shortly, the student was able to achieve the goal. Since the teacher was interested in the method the student used to accomplish the task, the teacher sat down and listened as the student taught. Such exploration possibilities with computers are endless. Students with intense motivation and large amounts of time can easily be challenged to solve problems which the teacher may not have attempted. In this process, the student may learn something about the computer system which the teacher may not otherwise have found. Although the situation may appear to be a threat to the teacher's role in the classroom, it can be considered a valuable resource for the teacher.

A major goal of education is the ability to learn independently. A computer science course is a natural place for students to develop this ability. In fact, students can learn independently and will certainly do so in such a course if the right atmosphere exists. Two key elements make up this atmosphere—it is challenging to students yet supportive of attempts to solve the problems presented.

Computer science is a very unique course to teach. The instructor lectures for only a small amount of time and spends more time working with individual students or small groups. Students are inevitably forced to develop good independent work habits because very often after being assigned a problem, they are on their own to solve it. The instructor becomes more of a facilitator to their education, helping them resolve their problems, and guiding them in their attempts to understand a particular assignment.

And, isn't that what education is all about?

References

1. Brown, Marc H. "What to Do When Your Computer Students Know More Than You Do." *Computing Teacher* 9, no. 2 (October 1981): 41–45.
2. Chalgren, Bill. "Computer Programming Term Project for High School Students." *Computing Teacher* 9, no. 4 (December 1981): 40–42.
3. Conway, Richard, and Archer, James. *Programming for Poets: A Gentle Introduction Using BASIC.* Cambridge, Mass.: Winthrop Publishers, 1979.
4. Dwyer, Thomas A., and Critchfield, Margot. *BASIC and the Personal Computer.* Reading, Mass: Addison-Wesley Publishing Co., 1978.
5. Edwards, Judith. *Elements of Computer Careers.* Englewood Cliffs, N.J.: Prentice-Hall, 1977.
6. Golden, Neal. *Computer Programming in the BASIC Language.* 2d ed. New York: Harcourt Brace Jovanovich, 1981.
7. Howard, Jim. "What Is Good Documentation?" *Byte* 6, no. 3 (March 1981): 132ff.
8. *Mathematics Teacher* (Special on Microcomputers) 74, no. 8 (November 1981). Reston, Va.: National Council of Teachers of Mathematics.

9. Mauer, H. A., and Williams, M. R. *A Collection of Programming Problems and Techniques.* Englewood Cliffs, N.J.: Prentice-Hall, 1972.

10. Nevison, John. *Little Book of BASIC Style.* Reading, Mass.: Addison-Wesley Publishing Co., 1978.

11. Papert, Seymour. *Mindstorms.* New York: Basic Books, 1980.

12. Polya, George. *How to Solve It.* Garden City, N.Y.: Doubleday and Co., 1957.

13. Prigger, Preston B. "The Hollister Project—A Three-Year Computer Science Curriculum for Secondary Schools." *Computing Teacher* 7, no. 3 (December 1979–January 1980): 4–7.

14. Rogers, Jean B. *An Introduction to Computers and Computing.* Eugene, Ore.: International Council for Computers in Education, Department of Computer and Information Science, University of Oregon, 1981.

15. ———, and Austing, Dick. "Computer Science in Secondary Schools: Recommendations for a One-Year Course." In *Topics—Computer Education for Elementary and Secondary Schools.* New York: Association for Computing Machinery, Inc., 1980; pp. 48–54.

16. U.S. Department of Labor. *Occupational Outlook Handbook,* 1982–83 edition. Washington, D.C.: Government Printing Office, March 1982.

15. Computer Software in Education

Judith B. Edwards

What *is* "software"? Where do I get it? How do I know if it's any good? Educators ask all these questions, and more, at an early stage in the process of introducing computers into their schools. This article discusses these issues.

WHAT IS "SOFTWARE"?

Any computer, from the least expensive home microcomputer to the largest and most sophisticated computer system, is totally useless without software. "Software" is the inclusive term used to describe the collection of computer programs that control the "hardware." Whether the computer is being used to print paychecks, interact with a sixth grader in a multiplication drill, or play Mastermind in full color, it is always under the control of stored sets of previously written instructions, called programs.

Software naturally includes all the computer-based instruction programs available for classroom use—the simulations, games, drills, tutorials, and interactive exploratory programs that may be used in any subject area. The term also includes the programming tools and languages needed by the person who develops those computer-based instructional programs. If, for example, a teacher were to purchase a microcomputer for classroom use, he or she would want to be sure to also receive at least one programming language (such as BASIC or Pascal) and perhaps an author language (such as PILOT). A programming language such as BASIC or Pascal allows teachers or students to write their own computer programs to solve problems, play games, or teach concepts. An author language such as PILOT allows a nonprogrammer to create instructional materials within an already-existing structured program. The teacher would also want to be sure to receive any programs required to operate peripheral equipment (such as a Disk Operating System) or special features of the computer (such as High Resolution Graphics). Most computer vendors also offer editing or word processing (such as Electric Pencil) programs. These programs or software packages allow the most

137

effective use of the new microcomputer.

The software just described comes in any one of a variety of physical forms. The program ordered may be stored on a magnetic tape—a large reel for a large computer or an ordinary small tape cassette for a microcomputer. It may be on a disk—from a small, five-inch-diameter flexible "floppy" disk to an eight-inch floppy disk, or even a large "hard" disk. Most recently, software is being offered as "firmware"; unlike the software on tape or disk which can be altered, the firmware program is permanently and *unalterably* stored on a plug-in ROM (Read-Only Memory) chip or cartridge. This firmware approach to programs is exemplified by the micro-computer which offers a wide selection of "plug-in" videogames.

To review and summarize, software is the term for all the pro-grams used to operate a computer with its peripheral equipment and to give it instructions. The programs themselves may be tools or languages to aid the programmer. Or, they may be applications such as computer-assisted instruction, games, financial accounting, stu-dent grade reporting, or statistical analysis. Or, they may be pro-grams the computer requires for the operation of its peripheral equipment or its special features. The software (programs) may be stored and delivered on a magnetic tape or disk, or on a permanent plug-in "chip."

WHERE IS SOFTWARE AVAILABLE?

Most teachers who are using a computer in the classroom have become adept at tracking down good programs or developing their own, or both. An increasing amount of instructional software is becoming available from commercial vendors and a variety of non-commercial sources, however. Commercial sources include, first and most importantly, the vendor who sells the particular computer being used. Although companies vary widely in the quantity and quality of the software they offer, the hardware vendor should never-theless be the first point of contact in searching for good software. (Many vendors have a toll-free number to call for help or informa-tion about software.) Several vendors offer a complete hardware/ software package for computer-assisted instruction—usually at a rel-atively high price. Notable examples of vendors providing complete software for instruction in conjunction with hardware are the Com-puter Curriculum Corporation (CCC) and Control Data Corporation (which markets the Plato software).

A second major source of software is established publishers, such as TimeShare and Milliken, which offer instructional software that will run on several different computers. A large number of smaller independent software vendors have emerged since the microcomputer became popular in schools, but the educator may find it difficult to evaluate the smaller company's ability to "service" the software should problems to found in the program. It is also difficult to predict the quality of a program to be obtained from an unknown vendor.

Other commercial or semicommercial software sources include computer stores, printed magazines, and "cassette magazines" in which programs are delivered on cassette tape. Computer stores, now a familiar sight in any moderate-size city, sell computer software off the shelf—usually on cassette or "floppy" disk. The customer can request a demonstration before buying, thus eliminating some risk and uncertainty. Most stores will order software if it is not in stock.

A selected list of some of the most popular printed computer magazines and computer "cassette magazines" appears in Appendix A. Each of the cassette magazines includes listings of a variety of useful, usually general interest, programs. Most of these cassette-tape magazines are published for use with one specific microcomputer; but some, such as GAUDEUS, offer issues on cassettes for several different micros from which the subscriber can choose. Most of the printed computer magazines listed in Appendix A typically include in each issue one or two complete listings of general interest or educational programs. Programs obtained from either type of magazine are comparatively low in cost, but in the case of printed listings, the user must type the entire program into his/her own computer.

Noncommercial software sources are many. First, clearinghouses for computer-based instructional programs are beginning to appear. In higher education, CONDUIT is a software exchange for exemplary high-quality instructional programs. Until 1980, no similar central software exchange existed for precollege instructional programs. Recently, a K–12 exchange has been established at Northeast Regional Educational Laboratory. It is called MicroSIFT: *Microcomputer Software and Information For Teachers*. It plans to disseminate a few exemplary high-quality and well-documented programs, review a catalog listing, and make tested programs available commercially and noncommercially. Appendix B provides addresses for these clearinghouses.

Proliferating across the nation, on the tide of the burgeoning microcomputer industry, are local computer "users' groups" whose members share information, experience, and programs; these groups constitute an expanding source of assistance as well as software. Such groups form most commonly around a particular brand of micro-computer; the microcomputer vendor or manufacturer is therefore the most immediate source of information about local groups. A number of microcomputer manufacturers issue a periodical newsletter to their hardware purchasers, which includes updated information about users' groups. Local computer stores, clearinghouses such as MicroSIFT, and special projects such as those discussed below may also be useful sources of information about the locations of specific groups.

With the increase in educational interest in computers and in their instructional use, numerous wide-based projects have been funded by state and federal agencies for the collection, development, and dissemination of instructional software. These projects, such as Minnesota Educational Computing Consortium (MECC) and Total Information for Educational Systems (TIES), are sources of a growing volume of instructional software. In addition, individual schools and universities around the country have been the site for developing considerable collections of instructional programs, and some of these have organized a formal process for offering their programs for sale to others. Like users' groups, most of these projects and school endeavors have at their base one or two specific brands of computers for which their software is designed; therefore program adaptation must be kept in mind by those seeking software for other computers or systems. For example, MECC has a substantial number of programs designed for use on Apple II microcomputers and another list of software for the CYBER 73 Timeshare System; Mounds View Public Schools in St. Paul, Minnesota, lists over 100 instructional programs designed for the PET microcomputer. In most cases, these projects and schools can provide catalogs of programs, price lists, and relevant information upon request. Appendix B includes selected lists of projects and school sources of programs with their addresses. An excellent source of information on computer-involved schools and projects is the *Academic Computing Directory* published by Human Resources Research Organization (1). It identifies over 300 U.S. schools, colleges, and universities that make significant use of computers for learning and teaching.

The most common source of software for educational computing during the last decade has been the individual instructor. With the command of an appropriate programming language, teachers, by and large, have found it quite effective to develop appropriate programs for use by their classes. Teachers with an appropriate instructional plan in mind, but without programming skills or time, have often obtained usable programs from other teachers or students with the needed skills and time. Friends and colleagues have also served as the source of already developed software for classroom use, although this means of exchange has been somewhat limited by the difficulties of transferability from one computer to another and by the wide variation in quality and completeness required by the developer/ teacher and that needed by the distant user/teacher. Teachers themselves and their colleagues and students will undoubtedly continue to be a major source of instructional programs as computers become an increasingly recognized subject and tool in progressive education.

HOW DO TEACHERS EVALUATE SOFTWARE?

An evaluation of instructional software for possible classroom use follows, in the main, the steps used for the evaluation of other clasroom materials with the addition of a few computer-specific questions to be answered. Because of the multimedia structure of computer-based educational units, however, teachers often find it helpful to order their evaluation steps more formally than is necessary with materials in simpler and/or more familiar formats. Examination copies and/or real-process examples are not readily available for computer-based instructional software. Thus printed descriptions, promotional materials and demonstrations, and verbal communications are the sources of information on which to base initial evaluation decisions.

In nearly all cases, the first steps in selection will address the essential questions of suitability of subject matter, grade level, pedagogical approach, and instructional goals, and will be automatic. In addition, computer-based materials require several computer-specific decisions concerning usability such as the following:

- Will the program run on my computer without significant modification?
- Is the computer/user dialogue clear and easy enough to understand so that my students can use it with little difficulty? Does the dialogue make clear how, when, and in what form user responses are to be entered? (For example, are there clear "prompts" with adequate indication of numeric or alpha input where required?)
- Are there, at least, sufficient basic operating instructions for the teacher?

For large, comprehensive software packages such as the CCC and Plato instructional programs or special curriculum packages such as Milliken's "Math Sequences," the software vendor can usually supply sufficient samples, introductory materials, and evaluation data on use and effectiveness to allow teachers to determine initially their possible appropriateness for their classes. It is also wise to add to vendor reports personal contacts with a sample of current users for their evaluation of the strengths and weaknesses of the software and its performance as an instructional medium. Vendors will ordinarily be able to provide such references, as will professional colleagues.

For smaller instructional programs and units, particularly those available from the increasing numbers of new vendors or individual program developers, there is little published data available to inform or guide the prospective instructional user. Teachers must rely on the casual program reviews published in the computer and instructional magazines such as those given in Appendix A, word-of-mouth critiques, user group reports, and reviews from established or informal clearinghouses.

Once teachers have answered these basic initial questions in the affirmative, they may wish to obtain copies of the unit materials not previously in hand and go on to evaluate additional concerns such as the hands-on operation of the program, its pedagogical usefulness, and the quality of the documentation and support materials.

Some of the most important questions regarding pedagogy for computer-based instructional units are the following:

- To what extent does the unit enhance or enrich classroom instruction?
- Does the unit provide experience which can be fitted into the existing course materials?
- To what extent does the unit provide students with an understanding of the learning objectives and a knowledge of how well they are achieving the objectives?
- What is the range of options for curricular use offered by the unit?
- What computer-related skills are prerequisite for effective student use of the unit?

Too frequently, documentation is not supplied with instructional programs, which in itself may present questions of supplementation. Where documentation is available to support the program, key questions will center on the adequacy of teacher support material, the appropriateness and completeness of student material, and the existence of a program listing and flowchart or description of logic flow.

An important consideration for teachers using computers in instruction is the effective evaluation of materials. Computer-based instructional units and programs, and complete curricular packages are beginning to appear in large numbers at all levels of completeness and quality. Several current textbooks contain a comprehensive and useful treatment of evaluation of such materials. Two of these are particularly recommended as references for the interested teacher: *Computer Applications in Instruction: A Teacher's Guide to Selection and Use*, pp. 74–105 (4), and *Learning Alternatives in U.S. Education: Where Student and Computer Meet*, pp. 375–91 (2). The most valuable new guide for evaluating instructional software in all fields is *Guidelines for Evaluating Computerized Instructional Materials* (3).

References

1. Human Resources Research Organization. *Academic Computing Directory.* Alexandria, Va.: Human Resources Research Organization, 1977.
2. Hunter, Beverly, et al. *Learning Alternatives in U.S. Education: Where Student and Computer Meet.* Englewood Cliffs, N.J.: Educational Technology Publications, 1975.
3. National Council of Teachers of Mathematics. *Guidelines for Evaluating Computerized Instructional Materials.* Reston, Va.: The Council, 1981.
4. Northwest Regional Educational Laboratory, TimeShare. *Computer Applications in Instruction: A Teacher's Guide to Selection and Use.* Boston: Houghton-Mifflin, TimeShare, 1978.

APPENDIX A

Selected List of Computer Magazines

Printed Magazines

Creative Computing, P.O. Box 789-M, Morristown, NJ 07960 (includes catalog)

BYTE, P.O. Box 361, Arlington, MA 02174

Journal of Computer-Based Instruction, 215 Southmain, Clarion, Iowa 50525

Microcomputing, Peterborough, NH 03458

On Computing, 70 Main Street, Peterborough, NH 03458

Recreational Computing, People's Computer Co., 1263 El Camino Real, Box E, Menlo Park, CA 94025

The Computing Teacher, Department of Computer and Information Sciences, University of Oregon, Eugene, OR 97403

THE Journal (Technological Horizons in Education), Information Synergy, Inc., 409 Massachusetts Ave., Acton, MA 01720

PET Gazette, 1929 Northport Dr., Room 6, Madison, WI 53704

RAINBOW: The Newsletter for Apple III owners, Box 43, Audubon, PA, 19407

Cassette Magazines

CURSOR, Box 550, Coleta, CA 93017 (PET)

CLOAD, Box 1267, Goleta, CA 93017 (TRS-80)

GAUDEUS, Box 113, Ozone Park, NY 11417 (PET, TRS-80, Apple II, Sorcerer)

APPENDIX B

Clearinghouses

CONDUIT (Clearinghouse—University Level), P.O. Box 388, Iowa City, Iowa 52244

MicroSIFT (Clearinghouse—K-12), Northwest Regional Educational Laboratory, 710 S.W. Second Ave., Portland, OR 97204

Selected Projects and Schools

Huntington II Project, c/o Dr. Lud Braun, State University of New York, Stonybrook, NY 11794

Minnesota Educational Computing Consortium (MECC), 2520 Broadway Dr., Lauderdale, MN 55113

Project LOCAL, 200 Nahatan St., Westwood, MA 02090

Total Information for Educational Systems (TIES), 1925 West County Rd. B-2, Roseville, MN 55113

Mounds View Public Schools, 2959 N. Hamline Ave., St. Paul, MN 55113, Attention: Sharon Conlan

University of California, Lawrence Hall of Science, Berkeley, CA 94702

University of Illinois, Computer-Based Education Research Lab (PLATO Project), Urbana, IL 61801

University of Oregon, Computer Science Department, Eugene, OR 97403, Attention: Dr. Dave Moursund

16. Selecting Microcomputers for the Classroom*

Donald H. McClain and David B. Thomas

Microcomputers suitable for serious instructional applications in the classroom are now available from a number of responsible manufacturers. Teachers have discovered microcomputers. They see them as an inexpensive way to provide computer-assisted instruction, computer literacy, data analysis, and other computer activities to students in the classroom. Many have rushed to buy one of the systems now available, often encouraged by administrators, parents, or school board members. Some of these purchasers will find that they soon outgrow their systems or that their systems do not serve their instructional needs.

Selecting an instructional computer system from the large number and variety of microcomputers now available can be a challenging venture even for an individual who is knowledgeable about instructional computing. But for the administrator or teacher who is not knowledgeable about computing, it can be a dilemma. The key to successful microcomputer selection lies in the careful analysis of the instructional problem, the determination of instructional requirements, and the specification of the required computing capability. Once the potential buyer has determined the computing capability, she or he can survey the marketplace for systems satisfying the specified needs. The final task is to select the system that satisfies all the predetermined criteria.

The purpose of this article is to guide the educator in selecting a computer system, especially a microcomputer system, for instruction. It describes a model and outlines a procedure to help teachers perform the prerequisite activities for specifying a microcomputer system which will meet their present and future needs.

*This article is based on a paper in the *AEDS Proceedings: 17th Annual Convention* (1979). A more extensive presentation of the ideas given here appeared in the *AEDS Journal* (Winter 1979). The authors wish to thank the editors of the *AEDS Journal* for permission to reproduce Figure 1 and Table 1 from the previous article.

The importance of analyzing the instructional needs and anticipated uses of the computer cannot be overemphasized. Microcomputers do not support the same levels of instructional computing as
existing large systems (or *mini*computers) do. Microcomputers can
be valuable additions to an instructional program, but careful planning will avoid the disappointment which can result from selecting
an inappropriate system.

THE MICROCOMPUTER SELECTION MODEL

Very often, one begins with the purchase of a computer or a
computer terminal intended for instructional use, and then attempts
to determine the applications of the new equipment. We suggest
that this approach is backward, that one should begin by identifying
instructional problems for which various forms of computing may
offer solutions. A five-phase model, depicted by Figure 1, provides a
systematic approach to selecting a microcomputer to meet present
and anticipated instructional needs. (N.B.: Many of our analyses
inevitably lead to the selection of microcomputers. Obviously, most
instructional problems will not lead to a computer solution.)

Identifying Instructional Problems

Individualized instructional programs often require the teacher to
spend time with diverse student ability-groups in the classroom.
Some students may work on vocabulary, while others work on grammar, math facts, chemical symbols, or spelling. Some students need
the opportunity to recite, to explain, or to ask questions. The computer has much to offer the teacher as a tool to facilitate the learning
of facts or principles and as an aid to problem solving. It can be an
effective resource freeing the teacher to concentrate on learning
activities requiring personal interaction. It is important to identify
the specific learning activity and a potential computer application
early in the selection process. We see the computer as a tool which
amplifies the teacher's effectiveness. But the teacher, as the responsible professional, must recognize the unique instructional problem
for which a computer solution is available. The teacher who realizes
that a group of students will profit from interactive drill, on punctu-
ation skills, for example, has completed the first step in the microcomputer selection process. Problems associated with the application of rules, or verbal associations, or concept learning can also be
mentioned. The teacher's problem identification process can identify
many areas where computing can provide help with the learning
process. Selecting the appropriate computing tool to solve the prob-

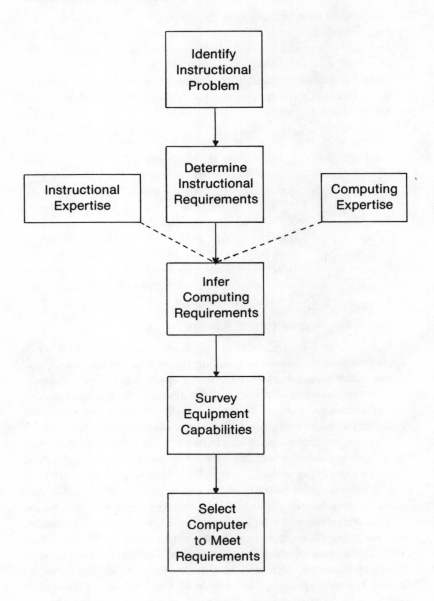

FIGURE 1
MICROCOMPUTER SELECTION MODEL

lem will yield more satisfaction than fitting the problem to the tool already selected.

Determining Instructional Requirements

After identifying the instructional problem, the teacher can then select a teaching strategy appropriate for the student. Eleven activities have been identified which represent the majority of suitable microcomputer applications. Administrative applications are excluded because they are not instructional in nature. These activities are as follows:

1. Drill-and-Practice exercises
2. Tutorial programs
3. Problem Solving exercises
4. Programming problems
5. Simulations
6. Interactive Testing sessions
7. Computer-Managed Instruction
8. Data Analysis exercises
9. Information Retrieval
10. Word Processing activities
11. Computer Literacy activities

Each of these activities or teaching strategies has associated characteristics which describe the instructional milieu. For example, feedback is descriptive of drill but not of data analysis; tutorials are characterized by interaction, but computer literacy activities are not. Eleven characteristics which describe the eleven strategies have also been identified. These characteristics are not exhaustive, but they represent the major instructionally oriented concerns associated with the activities listed.

The eleven characteristics of the instructional "contact" and the eleven strategies can be formed into an Instructional Requirements Matrix as shown in Table 1. The intersection of a strategy and a characteristic indicates a requirement which will later be translated into a computing requirement. The problem-solving strategy may be illustrative—neither high student terminal time nor significant interaction typically takes place within a problem-solving program; graphics may be necessary for some applications—for example, studying the shapes of mathematical functions. The entries in Table 1 are intended to be illustrative rather than prescriptive. Individual teachers should derive their own instructional requirements matrices which reflect their unique needs.

149

TABLE 1

INSTRUCTIONAL REQUIREMENTS MATRIX

Characteristic \ Strategy	Drill	Tutorial	Problem Solving	Programming	Simulation	Testing	CMI	Data Analysis	Information Retrieval	Word Processing	Computer Literacy
Interaction	X	X			X	X	X	X	X	X	X
Lower case		X			X	X				X	
Graphics		X	X		X	X		X			
Large Data Source		X			X	X	X		X	X	
Specific Language			X	X							X
Multiple Languages				X							
Student Record-keeping	X	X				X	X				
High Student Terminal Time		X		X	X					X	
Large Amount of Text		X		X	X			X	X	X	
Hard Copy Printed Output			X	X	X	X	X	X	X	X	X
Packaged Statistical Programs			X					X	X		

In identifying strategies it is important to take a fairly liberal view, considering the relative frequency of each strategy's use, and predicting strategies which may be used in the future. This analysis will be subjective, but it will provide weightings for the various characteristics. These subjective weights are used during a subsequent phase of the selection procedure to develop specific computing requirements.

Teachers can use the Instructional Requirements Matrix to focus the needs of the various strategies. By collapsing across strategies, they obtain a list of the instructional requirements which the computing equipment must satisfy.

The remainder of this article describes the general capabilities or options of microcomputers believed to be essential in considering an instructional computing system. Further, it relates these capabilities to the various instructional activities or strategies that teachers may wish to use.

MICROCOMPUTER CAPABILITIES

At the heart of every microcomputer is the microprocessor, the part of the system that manipulates all information and performs all calculations. Microprocessors are available from numerous manufacturers, each processor having a different instruction set and either 8- or 16-bit word lengths. Each of these different processors has sufficient power, speed, and precision for most instructional applications, so that its brand name is less important in selecting an instructional computer than some of the other features.

The instructional programs and data being processed by the microcomputer are stored in the memory unit. Memory is a vital resource of the microcomputer and the size of usable memory is a very important factor in determining the types of instructional computing that can be accomplished. Drill-and-practice and computer literacy programs usually utilize amounts of memory in the 4,000- to 8,000-character range, problem solving and programming applications under 8,000 characters. Thirty-two thousand characters are normally sufficient for tutorials and simulations, but in some cases more may be required. Two points concerning memory should be considered when purchasing a system: (1) How much memory quoted by the manufacturer for the system is actually available for the application? (2) What is the maximum amount of memory that can be supported by the system? The ability to add additional memory permits room for expansion.

Another capability to consider is the character set. Many microcomputers have only uppercase letters. For most instructional applications other than problem solving and programming, it is desirable to have both upper- and lowercase. Almost all other student learning materials make use of both cases and educators should not settle for less in instructional computing. Further, the character size as well as the availability of special characters should be noted. In certain applications, the ability for the user to design an alternate character set may be an asset and should be kept in mind.

In conjunction with the character set, two other factors to weigh in the selection process are the number of characters per line and the number of lines per display. The number of lines per display depends upon the display unit used by the system. Too small a number of display lines can limit the types of instructional applications implemented. Tutorials, simulations, and programming applications require the largest number of lines per display—24 lines are probably sufficient. Also, the number of characters per line can limit what can be printed efficiently and readably. A recommended size for most instructional applications is approximately 60 characters per line.

Every instructional system must have some external storage device for keeping the curriculum materials and associated programs. Usually, this storage medium is either a cassette tape or a floppy diskette. The cassette tape units use typical audiotapes; their contents are transferred to the computer through a regular tape recorder. The floppy diskette is a thin, circular magnetic recording surface enclosed in a square envelope with an exposed recording area. The information on a diskette is read into the computer's memory by a disk drive. Tape recorders are inexpensive but slow and read information only in a sequential order. Disk devices, on the other hand, are more expensive but much faster and can read information from anywhere on the diskette. Therefore, if the instructional setting requires several different programs to be available on demand, the disk capability is recommended.

Many microcomputers have a graphics capability integrated within the system. In some systems, this feature even includes up to 15 different colors. The ability to do graphical representations and to use color can be extremely helpful in almost all types of instructional computing, particularly drill-and-practice, tutorial, and simulations.

Two other features that may be advantageous in some instructional settings are the existence of other programming languages and the ability to utilize the microcomputer as a terminal to another computer.

Almost every microcomputer has available the programming language BASIC, but many also have available other programming languages which may be necessary in teaching computer science or computer literacy courses. Further, the ability to use the microcomputer as a terminal into a larger computer system may permit using the larger system to develop materials and then transferring the resulting programs into the memory of the microcomputer. Also, the system can be used in a hierarchical arrangement—using the microcomputer as a stand-alone system for most instructional computing, but using the larger system when more resources are required. In a setting where the user has access to other computer systems either locally or through a network, it is recommended that the microcomputer be equipped with a communication interface, permitting use as a terminal.

The last capability of microcomputers to be discussed is the ability to directly connect peripherals, expanding the system's potential. Peripherals that are extremely beneficial in instructional computing are printers, plotters, graphic input tablets, music boards, speech synthesizers, speech recognition systems, random access audio devices, random access slide projectors, and video disk players. A microcomputer with the flexibility to permit connection of a selection of peripherals should be viewed favorably. When comparing peripherals, make sure that software is available to support them in the particular micro and that their addition will not require a major rewrite of existing courseware. The addition of other media to the instructional computing applications can greatly enhance effectiveness.

In completing the selection process, be sure to compile a set of computing requirements in conjunction with the identified instructional requirements. Then, survey the market, matching those capabilities and systems which satisfy the computing requirements previously determined. Table 2 illustrates an example survey of some of the more popular microcomputer systems and their capabilities. During this phase, consult individuals who own microcomputers, computer stores which sell several different systems, computing magazines which evaluate various systems, and other schools concerning their firsthand experience with the potential systems. The selection of a microcomputer which will be responsive to the needs and the requirements identified can now follow. Teachers following the proposed model can be confident that the selected microcomputer will support their instructional computing applications. A computer system which meets present and future needs will do much to assure a successful instructional computing experience.

TABLE 2

Comparison of Microcomputer Systems

Capabilities \ System	Apple II	ATARI 400	ATARI 800	TRS-80 III	TRS-80 Color	MONROE EC8800	IBM	CBM 8032	TI 99/4A	Osborn I	Heath Z-89
Processor	6502	6502	6502	Z80A	6809E	Z80A	8088	6502	TMS9900	Z80A	Z80
Memory Minimum/Maximum	16/64	8/16	16/48	4/48	4/32	128/128	16/256	32/32	16/48	64/64	48/64
Lowercase	YES[2]	YES	YES	YES[3]	NO	YES	YES	YES	NO	YES	YES
Display Included	NO	NO	NO	YES	NO	NO	NO	YES	NO	YES	YES
Disk Drive Included	NO	NO	NO	NO	NO	YES	NO	NO	NO	YES	YES
Graphics Resolution (Vert x Horiz)	40 x 48 / 192 x 280	96 x 160 / 192 x 320	192 x 320	48 x 128	32 x 64 / 192 x 256	78 x 80 / 240 x 240	200 x 640 / 200 x 320	25 x 80	256 x 192	34 x 128	24 x 80
Text (Lines x Characters)	24 x 40	24 x 40	24 x 40	16 x 64/32	16 x 32	24 x 40	25 x 80	25 x 80	24 x 32	24 x 52	24 x 80
Communications Included (RS-232C)	NO	NO	NO	NO	YES	YES	NO	NO	NO	YES	YES
Multiple Languages	YES	YES	YES	YES	NO	YES	YES	YES[2]	YES	YES[2]	YES[2]
Sound	YES	YES	YES	NO	YES	YES	YES	NO	YES	NO	NO
Special Features	4/15 Colors	16 Colors Program Cart. I/O Port	16 Colors Program Cart. I/O Port	Integra. System Printer Interface	8 Colors Program Cart.	8 Colors 3 RS232 Ports	16 Colors	IEEE Interface 128 Graphic Char.	16 Colors	Complete System in Case Dual Drive	Kit Available for 1895
Cost[1]	1330	399	899	699	399	2996	1565	1495	525	1795	2895

[1] Manufacturer's suggested price for minimum configuration
[2] Available from other than manufacturer
[3] Only with model III BASIC

The Contributors

David H. Ahl, a pioneer in the field of computer simulations and games, is the author or editor of 7 books and over 100 articles and papers on computer applications. He is publisher of *Creative Computing,* the trend-setting magazine in software applications for home and school. He spends a great deal of time working with school-age students on computing and independent learning.

Bob Albrecht, Louise Burton, and **Ramon Zamora,** sometimes known as the Dragons of Menlo Park (California), are among the most creative computer educators in the country. The originators of several popular computer magazines, including *Recreational Computing* (recently merged with *Compute*), they have also written numerous books and articles on computers and BASIC programming for children and adults.

Ronald E. Anderson is an Associate Professor of Sociology at the University of Minnesota, and Project Director of the Minnesota Educational Computing Consortium project "Instructional Materials for Computer Literacy," funded by the National Science Foundation. He is the author of numerous articles on instructional computing and computer literacy and is a series editor for CONDUIT.

Bruce E. Brombacher, 1982 National Teacher of the Year, is a mathematics teacher and department chairperson at Jones Junior High School, Upper Arlington, Ohio. He spearheaded the drive for the use of microcomputers in the classroom and served as chairperson of the district computer services committee. As a member of the School Study Council of Ohio's Microcomputer and Technology Commission, he presents microcomputer workshops and is involved in in-service for district instructional staff implementing the microcomputer as an instructional tool in the classroom.

J. Richard Dennis is an Associate Professor of Secondary Education at the University of Illinois, where he has pioneered in models for training computer-using teachers. Since 1963, he has been involved in computer-based education and mathematics education. He is the editor of a series of publications on training teachers to use computers.

Judith B. Edwards is Director of the Computer Technology Program, including the Microcomputer Software and Information For Teachers (MicroSIFT) clearinghouse, at the Northwest Regional Educational Laboratory in Portland, Oregon. She has been actively involved in instructional computing since the 1960's.

Linda Borry Hausmann, a former junior high school music and mathematics teacher, has been actively involved in intructional computing for the past eleven years, six of them at the Minnesota Educational Computing Consortium. Currently she is the manager of instructional systems for EduSystems, responsible for curriculum development, program development, and in-service activities. She is a coauthor of the Apple Music Theory package and the MECC arithmetic drill and practice set.

Mel Hynek is a curriculum specialist for business education in the Milwaukee Public Schools. During most of his teaching career, he taught computer-related aspects of business education.

Henry S. Kepner, Jr., is Professor of Curriculum and Instruction, responsible for computer and mathematics education, at the University of Wisconsin–Milwaukee. He is a frequent contributor to educational journals, and served on the NCTM Interpretive Report Committee on the National Assessment of Educational Progress in Mathematics, which included reports on student knowledge and attitudes about computers.

Daniel L. Klassen is Director of Academic Computing and Educational Research at St. Olaf College, Northfield, Minnesota. Formerly the Director of the Special Projects Division, Minnesota Educational Computing Consortium, he also worked at the Northwest Regional Educational Laboratory developing computer-based learning materials and a teacher guide to computers in instruction. His experience also includes work on the Huntington Computer Project, where he developed computer-based instructional simulations.

Joseph W. Kmoch is computer science and mathematics teacher at Washington High School, Milwaukee's computer specialty school, where he teaches students, from beginners to advanced, programming and computer science. One of his students won the 1979 AEDS National Computer Programming Contest.

Donald H. McClain is Computer-Based Educational Specialist in the Instructional Services Division of the Weeg Computing Center at the University of Iowa.

Vincent F. O'Connor is the mathematics curriculum specialist for the Milwaukee Public Schools. He is also chairperson of the district instructional computing committee, and is involved in training elementary, middle, and senior high school teachers in using computers. A former president of the Wisconsin Mathematics Council, he conducts computer workshops for the council and for the National Council of Teachers of Mathematics.

Don G. Rawitsch is the manager of user services for the Minnesota Educational Computing Consortium. He is codeveloper of the widely used Oregon Trail simulation, and has conducted workshops on computer use at national, regional, and state social studies conferences.

Eric P. Schluter is mathematics department chairperson and a teacher in the computer data processing career specialty program at Washington High School, Milwaukee. His experience includes on-site training in business data processing.

Ron Tenison, a science teacher at Catlin Gable School in Portland, Oregon, established a computer curriculum for science students starting in the ninth grade, and has spearheaded computer use in the schools during the last decade. He served as president of the Oregon Council for Computers in Education, the founding group of *The Computing Teacher.*

David B. Thomas is Associate Research Scientist in the CAI Laboratory and Instructional Services Division of the Weeg Computing Center at the University of Iowa.

WESTMAR COLLEGE LIBRARY

About This Book

Computers in the Classroom provides teachers at all levels an introduction to computer uses—both planned and current—for classroom instruction. The book focuses on instructional use rather than on recordkeeping, budget, and management. It is divided into three parts: Educational Uses of Computers, The Computer in the Curriculum, and Computer Equipment and Materials.

Among the educational issues discussed are instructional applications of computers, computer literacy, computer games, the computer and exceptional children. The book considers computer use in the elementary school and in the following curriculum areas: language arts and reading, social studies, fine arts, business education and careers, science, middle school and senior high school mathematics. It also offers teachers suggestions for designing and teaching a secondary school course in computer science. The third part of the book provides practical recommendations and guidelines for selection and use of computer software and microcomputers in the classroom.

Contributors to this book in NEA's Developments in Classroom Instruction series write from their own knowledge of and experience with computers. They include authors who work with computers in all areas of instruction from elementary school to university level, editors of computing magazines, and staff members of a state educational computing consortium.